MY SON, MY SON, WHERE ARE YOU?

A SOLDIER'S LIFE IN THE 12TH INFANTRY REGIMENT

WILLIAM J. BROWN

To My Darling Wife
Mary Ann

©2016 by W. J. Brown
All rights reserved. No part of this publication may be reproduced or transmitted in any form or by any means, electronic or mechanical, including photocopy, recording, or any information storage and retrieval system, without the prior written permission of the publisher.

Front Cover Description

Front cover jacket displays a photo of Frank W. Brown holding his M-1 Garand Rifle surrounded with the 1944 American Flag and the Purple Heart. Frank Brown Archives

Purple Heart, awarded by the United States Armed Forces for being wounded or killed in any action against an enemy of the United States or as a result of an act of any such enemy or opposing armed forces. Frank Brown Archives

Table of Contents

Dedication.................................5		
Acknowledgements..............................6		
Forward....................................7		
Chapter One	Origins....................9	
Chapter Two	The Early Years.............15	
Chapter Three	Young Manhood..............22	
Chapter Four	Induction..................27	
Chapter Five	Camp Croft.................30	
Chapter Six	Ft. Devens to Dix to Benning..41	
Chapter Seven	Camp Gordon................50	
Chapter Eight	Carolina Maneuvers..........66	
Chapter Nine	Return to Camp Gordon.......74	
Chapter Ten	Fort Dix...................99	
Chapter Eleven	Camp Gordon Johnston.......112	
Chapter Twelve	Fort Jackson...............122	
Chapter Thirteen	England...................129	
Chapter Fourteen	Normandy D-Day............154	
Chapter Fifteen	No Word...................167	
Chapter Sixteen	Coming Home...............179	
Epilogue.................................191		
Notes & Photo Credits 194		
Appendix A	Frank's Timeline of Service 196	
Appendix B	Frank's Cartoons...........197	
Appendix C	Letter from Sgt. Ed Phillips...217	
Appendix D	Letter from Lt. Forbes......218	
	About the Author..........221	

Dedication

THIS BOOK IS DEDICATED TO THE THOUSANDS OF MILITARY SERVICE, MEN AND WOMEN, WHO GAVE THE ULTIMATE SACRIFICE IN WWII AND TO ALL THE FAMILIES ON THE HOME FRONT, WHO SUFFERED THE PAIN OF THEIR LOSS.

"****"

Acknowledgements

The author would be remiss if he did not acknowledge the support of his loving wife, Mary Ann, who offered encouragement throughout the writing of this book.

The author's family and friends for their helpful comments during the initial draft review.

The Camp Gordon Johnston Association for their photo contributions on the amphibious training conducted at the camp during WWII.

Eleanor (Thielman) Peinkofer for corresponding as a pen pal with my brother in WWII. She found letters from Frank in 2004 and through her inquiry she became known to the surviving family members and shared her experience and letters with the family and the Jell-O Museum.

The Jell-O Corporation, when owned by General Foods, for their support of the soldiers in WWII, who were employed by the company when they entered military service. They continued to receive annual bonuses, and goodwill packages throughout their service time.

"*****"

FORWARD

I have for some time wanted to document the life of my brother, Frank W. Brown, who served and was killed in action in World War II. This short story is an attempt to accomplish this for future generations to fully understand and appreciate the sacrifice of those who gave their lives and the effect on the family back home.

I never got to know my brother well, since the year I was born in 1935, the same year he graduated from Le Roy High School in Le Roy, NY. Although he lived at home for six years after my birth, I was just too young to capture a memory of him before his entry into military service. The few details I do remember I will certainly include in this story. So this has been an adventure to discover as many details as I could about a young man with noble aspirations caught in a world war and its effect on him and his family.

Much of this story is rendered in letters, photos and several documents that I found in my mother's possessions. Frank and his mother had a very close relationship, and they corresponded about two to three times per week. She saved all of his letters, around 500, and this was a valuable asset in writing this book. The content of his letters depict life in the army in the 1941 to 1944 period and reflect the life of the family on the home front, stressed by the war and having a loved one in harms way. These correspondences reveal his outstanding character, concern for others, and intense spirituality, throughout his military career. Daily, he showed his spirituality in his belief in God, accepting God's will and the hardships of a soldier's life with optimism and a heartfelt joy.

When D-Day occurred, June 6, 1944, word was lost from Frank and a period of two months passed without knowing Frank's whereabouts or his condition. The only information they had was the daily war news. His mother and father had no knowledge that he was killed in action on June 8th and would not have official notification until August 6, 1944. Information traveled much slower than today, requiring months instead of minutes. When news did arrive, it was many times incomplete, uncertain and confusing, leaving loved ones not knowing the state of their soldier.

If my brother were alive today, May 20, 2016, he would be 98 years old. I can only imagine his legacy and contributions to society. However, it was God's will that he would make the ultimate sacrifice for his country by giving his life in combat so we can enjoy our precious freedoms to this day.

Let us never forget the sacrifice of all our military service men and women and their families in past and present wars. May these memories motivate us to appreciate and exercise our freedoms to our fullest extent. God will bless America when we honor Him.

Isaiah 26:3-4, "You will keep in perfect peace him whose mind is steadfast because he trusts in you. Trust in the Lord forever, for the Lord, the Lord, is the Rock eternal."

"****"

Chapter One

Origins
1847 to 1917

Frank's grandparents on his father's side originated from Northern Italy. His Grandfather, Charles Baroncini, was born in 1847 in Cremona, Italy while his Grandmother Maria (Mary) Cingnetta was born in 1848 somewhere in Northern Italy. They had three children born in Italy; Frank on January 7, 1874, Giovanni (John) on March 20, 1879, and Charles on July 3, 1883. They applied for immigration to America and made the great voyage across the Atlantic around 1883 - 1884 with only a few trunks holding their limited possessions. When they arrived, New York City must have been overwhelming to them, and Grandpa Charles tried to find work that would pay for food and meager lodging. Jobs were very scarce, and he soon reached the conclusion that there was much discrimination because of their Italian heritage. Since they came from Northern Italy, their appearance could pass as an Austrian because of their light colored skin; therefore, he decided to change the family name to Brown because of the familiar sound to Baroncini. Of course, there was no money for legal change, so Brown it was on the spot! After about a year in New York City, he heard of work in a salt mine 26 miles southwest of Rochester, NY, near the village of Retsof, NY. As a matter of trivia, Retsof is the word Foster spelled backward who was the founder of the town. The mine became one of the world's largest salt mines and was active until 1994 when it started to collapse due to flooding by underground water. The original population was mostly of Italian origin where they lived in a company town in which the salt mine owned the houses and a store. The town is located near Cuylerville, NY, where in the colonial period a large Seneca Indian village existed called Little Beard's Town. When the family resided in

Retsof, Amelia was born on October 10, 1885, Francis (Fannie) on September 8, 1889, and Jacob (Jack) on January 4, 1891. Jacob would in time become Frank's father. After a few years time, Grandpa Charles decided to move to Buffalo, which was a growing city with plenty of work. Around the turn of the century, two of his sons, Frank and John, opened up a meat market in Buffalo, and their mother Mary cleaned out passenger train railroad cars.

Figure 1 Le Roy Homestead

Jack grew up in Buffalo and told of his experiences there hopping on streetcars to go to the Pan American Exposition in South Buffalo near Lake Erie. It wasn't long before the meat market failed, and the word was John and Frank were drinking up the profits. Frank contacted pneumonia and died at the age of 27 on October 21, 1901. Grandma Mary decided it would be better to move to the country, and it was their dream to buy a small plot of land for a farm. She saved her money and heard of the little town of Le Roy, NY, where a salt mine was abandoned, and the company was selling off the company houses. So they made the trip to Le Roy and bought two houses from the National Salt Company and 9 acres of land from Henry L. Johnson on November 14, 1904, for $450.00. The two houses were moved about a half-mile and attached at the 9 acres they now owned. The deed showed the property was placed in the name of Mary (Maria) Brown (Baroncini). Mary's name on the deed provides a clue on who was taking charge for the future homestead of the Brown family.

Figure 2 Charles & Mary Brown

Grandpa and Grandma Brown were well pleased in their new home, the first since Italy where they had lived in the poorest of conditions. In time, they bought chickens, a pig, a cow and a horse. On the front of the house, a porch was added and, a room back of the kitchen called the "back kitchen." At first, well water was manually pumped from a hand-dug well, and rainwater was collected from the roof gutters in a rain barrel. In the early 1920s, a barn was added where there was a stall for the cow and horse, and a chicken coup was added onto the barn. Apple, cherry, and pear trees were planted and a field of raspberry bushes. Grandpa Brown was known for grafting apple trees where three varieties of apples were being grown on the same tree. Two acres of grapes were planted in the early 1920's and were sold in the local Le Roy market.

On his mother's side, Frank's Grandpa, John (Giovanni) Stefani was born in Asiago, Italy, on May 12, 1863, which around that time was part of Austria. John was the first in his family to come to America in 1885.

Figure 3 John Stefani

He soon sent for his rest of his family to join him, which included mom, dad, six brothers, and sisters.

11

Grandma Johanna Kunego was born on June 24, 1874, in Forbach, Bavaria and came to America in 1887. Kunego then was spelled Cunico and was most likely misspelled on arrival in the USA. She was raised in Germany for thirteen years so she could only speak German.

Figure 4 Johanna Stefani

Upon arrival in the USA, they would usually travel by train to Lime Rock, N.Y, a small community in upstate New York. Many families immigrated from Asiago to Lime Rock, since their family members had settled there previously. There was work in the two limestone quarries just a few miles west and north of Lime Rock. In Lime Rock, there were kilns to heat limestone and produce lime, a very widely used product. Grandpa John married Grandma Johanna Kunego, in Piffard, N.Y, in 1888. John was not in the area long when he bought the property on the Gulf Road in Lime Rock in front of the limestone quarry next to the Lehigh Valley railroad tracks.

Figure 5 Stefani Gulf Hotel

The property was run as a boarding house and saloon for the quarry workers. As the Stefani family grew, the children, primarily women, worked in the boarding house changing beds, doing the laundry, fixing meals and tending the bar. At this time, the children were starting to leave home, and he did not have the free labor to continue operating a boarding house. Frank's mother, Nellie (Johanna), was the fourth daughter born, and when Katie the oldest left to work at a candy factory in Niagara Falls, she took Nellie with her much to the dismay of their father.

There were ten children: eight girls and two boys. In Figure 6 below is Katie, Lena, Mary, Tony, Nellie, Minnie in back row with Anna, Grandma Stefani, Lucy, Elizabeth, Grandpa Stefani, Mannie in front row.

Figure 6 John Stefani Family

When the Gulf Hotel burned in 1919, Grandpa Stefani moved his family to Lime Rock where he opened a grocery store on Route 5 next to the limekiln.

Figure 7 Stefani Grocery Store

Nellie met her husband James (also known as Jacob and later Jack) in 1915, when she was 19 years old. She was already dating another beau but when she met Jack she knew he was the one. They were married on March 1, 1916, and planned to use a brand new 1916 Model T Ford as the wedding car. Jack had just bought the car, and it was his pride and joy since very few people owned cars in

1916. However as fate would have it, there was a major snowstorm the day before the wedding, so the vehicle became a horse and sleigh, which got them to the church on time. Remember, in that day and age, there were no snowplows since there were few automobiles. Jack and Nellie took residence at the Warsaw Road homestead with her in-laws Charles and Mary Brown and cared for them until their death years later.

It wasn't long before Jack and Nellie's first child was born on May 27, 1917. They proudly named him Frank William Brown. Frank was the first of five children, three boys, and two girls.

Exodus 20:12, Honor your father and mother, so that you may live long in the land the Lord your God is giving you."

"****"

Chapter Two

The Early Years
1917 to 1935

Frank was born to Nellie (Johanna) and Jacob (Jack) Brown on May 27, 1917, at 8:40 O'clock at the home, 9500 Warsaw Road (Route 19), Le Roy, New York. He weighed eight pounds and was 21 inches long.

Figure 8 Baby Frank

His mother recorded the complete details in a baby booklet, which many parents typically have for their first-born. Here are some of the details as recorded in that booklet:

Born: May 27, 1917, at 8:40 AM at home
    Eight Pounds, 21 inches
Parents: Jacob and Nellie Brown
Grandparents: Charles & Mary Brown (Baroncini) and John & Johanna Stefani

Gifts: One gold ring, one toilet set, two bonnets, one dress, one sacque, one pair of booties, one pair of shoes, one pair of stockings.
Franks first laugh: five months old.
Franks first outing: July 4, 1917
Franks first short clothes: four months old.
Franks first picture: seven months old.
Franks first party: June 1917
Franks first words: Mama & Papa
Boyhood Events:
Three fingers were burnt in December 1917.
Leg broke on January 8, 1921.
Started school, District #11, Jug City, September 5, 1923.

In Figure 9, Mom was holding Frank at almost one-year-old in 1918. At this time, the American Expeditionary Force was ordered to aid the Allied Forces in Europe for World War I. Just 23 years later, this child would be serving in World War II, which in looking back was a continuance of the first war. Note the fruit trees that Grandpa Brown had planted in a well-manicured field.

Figure 9 Mom & Frank

Frank grew up on the small farm on Warsaw Road while his father worked at the Le Roy Plow Works as a cast iron molder. Frank's grandfather, Charles, worked the small 9-acre farm, which included chickens, a horse, a cow, and maybe a pig. Charles was an excellent fruit and vegetable farmer. He had at various times apples, pears, peaches, cherries, raspberries and a grape vineyard. Summers would always include a large vegetable garden with extra produce that he would sell in town. The following are pictures of the family, which tell the story better than words. Figure 10 is a picture of Grandpa Brown sawing wood, the primary fuel for cooking and heating in the cold winters in upper New York State.

Figure 10 Grandpa Brown Sawing Wood

The cow became well known in family storytelling because one day it became adventurous in escaping from the farm by taking the B&O railroad tracks south. Two or three days later the cow was found mired in mud at Beaver Meadow, about two miles from the farm. The cow was rescued, but it could no longer give any milk, so it was sold to another farmer. I hope that farmer knew what he was getting! Beef not milk.

Figure 11 Brown's Adventurous Cow

In 1921, their second child, Eleanor was born. Figure 12 is a picture of Frank, Mom, and Eleanor in front of the barn.

17

Figure 12 Frank, Mom, & Eleanor

The family grew quickly and by 1926, there were four children. The picture in Figure 13 was taken in 1926 at Jack's brothers home, the Valley Hotel. Frank was about nine years old here. The Valley Hotel and saloon was run by John and Mary Brown and was the talk of Le Roy since John and Mary would fight on a quite frequent basis, and alcohol certainly contributed to the problem. One day when the family was invited down for dinner, John and Mary got in a fight and Mary threw a plate of spaghetti at John and hit the doorway above him. He immediately wore the spaghetti on his head. Our family got up from the table and quickly left not to return for some time to come.

Figure 13 Frank, Mary, Mom, Eleanor, Al & Dad

18

In Figure 14, Frank is two years old in the front yard. Note the maple tree behind him. Grandpa trimmed the lower limbs so in later years the tree could be sold for lumber. The picture shows that the grass was not cut so the cow could pasture in the front yard.

Figure 14 Frank Two Years Old

Figure 15 shows Frank's brother Al with Frank taken in 1924. Frank looks like a typical farm boy while Al is ready to rumble.

Figure 15 Al & Frank 1924

Frank in uniform, Figure 16, was taken in 1924 and may have been his first holy communion since he would have been seven years old. Frank was raised Roman Catholic, attended public schools but received his religious education through the

Confraternity of Christian Doctrine (CCD) classes which would have been once per week during the school year. The family was active in the church and seldom missed Sunday mass.

Figure 16 Frank's First Holy Communion

Figure 17, a photo taken in 1928, shows Frank with his sister Mary at three years old, Jackie Brown a cousin at 10 and Al at seven years old. The family car in the background appears new and is likely a two door 1928 Model A Ford. Frank built himself a model airplane that he is very proud of, and the two boys are in the cowboy play gun stage. Frank had an early interest in airplanes when at that time the Le Roy Woodward Airport was in full operation. Being just a few miles from the airport, I'm sure many prop planes would fly overhead, and Frank would marvel at aviation on a daily occurrence. Later when Frank graduated from high school, he wanted to pursue a career in aeronautical engineering but the family did not have the money for college, so he was unable to attend. Don't you love those socks that Al has on?

Figure 17 Mary, Frank, Cousin Jackie & Al

In the summer of 1932, Frank in Figure 18 is shown with Al, Mary, and Eleanor. Frank was 15 years old ready to start his freshman year in high school. The grape vineyard in the background was planted in the early 1920s and provided ample Concord grapes for many years.

Figure 18 Frank, Al, Mary & Eleanor

The grapes were sold in the local Le Roy market and what was left was made into an Italian red wine sometimes referred to as Dago Red. This was a tart wine that warmed many a tummy in the cold winters. Dad would always have a decanter of wine when relatives or guests came to the homestead and plenty of food was always made available. Jack and Nellie were very responsible parents and took pride in their children in making sure they were obedient, had proper manners and did well in school. They wanted their children to have a better education and life than they were allowed to have in this great nation of ours.

Psalm 127:3, "Sons are a heritage from the Lord, children a reward from him."

"*****"

Chapter Three

Young Manhood
1935 to 1941

Frank spent his grade school years at District #11 in Jug City, N.Y., which is just a crossroad at a mile west of the homestead. The folklore was that jugs were made in the "city" many years ago and thus the name. The small one-room schoolhouse burned down in the late 1920s. A new one was built on the site at about the time Frank went to the local high school. The summer before starting high school he was encouraged to show responsibility in planting and maintaining a garden. One day in midsummer an agricultural agent paid a visit to review Frank's garden. He found the garden in tall weeds with hardly a vegetable to be seen, much to Frank's embarrassment. Frank's interest did not include gardening or any farm work. He hated to be called by the local farmer when it was harvest time, and a small amount of change could be made doing dirty labor such as threshing wheat. When he would come home, he would be covered in dust, and all you could see were his two blue eyes. Franks interest was in books. He read books whenever he could and loved making model airplanes. In the fall of 1931, he transferred to Le Roy High School and was an excellent student.

Figure 19 Frank's High School Graduation 1935

In those days, Latin was emphasized, and he ended up taking four years of the ancient language, which is hard to comprehend since he would never speak it. The Catholic mass was said in Latin, so maybe he could understand what the priest was saying. Frank would have taken the usual subjects such as four years of English, history, math and science. There were few electives in those days, but Latin was certainly one of them. Frank graduated in June 1935, in a class of 77 seniors.

Figure 20 High School Diploma

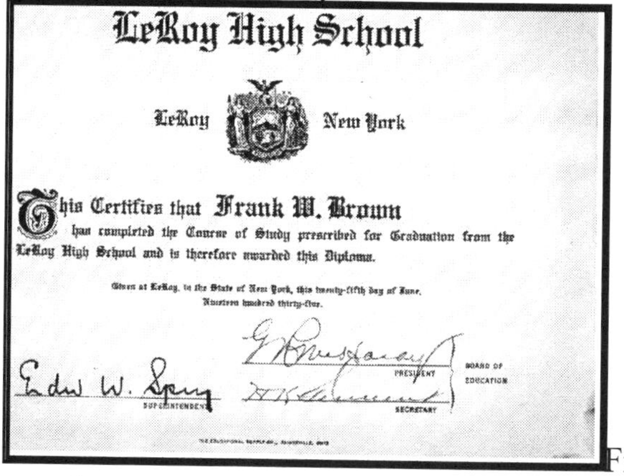

LeRoy High School

LeRoy New York

This Certifies that Frank W. Brown has completed the Course of Study prescribed for Graduation from the LeRoy High School and is therefore awarded this Diploma.

Given at LeRoy, in the State of New York, this twenty-fifth day of June, Nineteen hundred thirty-five.

SUPERINTENDENT

PRESIDENT

SECRETARY

BOARD OF EDUCATION

Frank was one of 36 seniors who made the Honor Roll for the 1935 school year. He also received the Samuel Mann Award for the excellence of character, which shows what an example he presented to the teachers and his peers at Le Roy High.

Figure 21 Samuel Mann Award

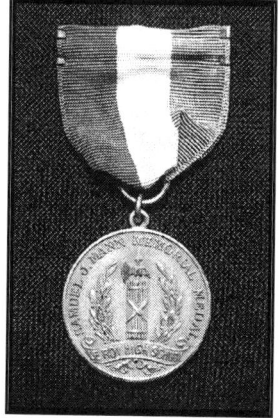

On Monday, June 24, the Senior Program was held, and there was a Panel Presentation on Three Hundred Years of Secondary Education in the United States, 1635 - 1935. Frank was on that panel and gave a presentation on the program and philosophy of secondary education. Mom said Frank was very nervous when he gave his talk since he was shy and not used to public speaking.

Interestingly, Frank was recommending that secondary education develop a curriculum in the trades as vocational schools.

Frank wanted to attend college pursuing a career in aeronautical engineering. His parents did not have the funds for college, but his Uncle Bill and Aunt Francis Ireland mentioned in his junior year, that they would help him with the finances. However, when high school graduation came there was no mention of providing any assistance. Scholarships were very few, and college loans were unknown. In 1935, Uncle Bill Ireland, a sales manager for the Todd Company, was making plans for manufacturing an electric pencil sharpener and needed to provide sufficient capital. As it turns out, a few years later in 1940 the federal government placed restrictions on metals due to the strong possibility of war. Bill Ireland lost all the capital he had invested in the ill-fated venture. So after graduation, since the country was in the middle of the Great Depression and jobs were very hard to find, Frank attended a vocational school in Rochester, NY, and received a trade certificate as a tin sheet metal worker. Frank was good at mathematics, especially geometry, and this was necessary for reading blueprints and making the tin products. In 1936, he got a job at the Jell-O Company plant in Le Roy as a tinsmith and worked there for five years until entering military service in 1941.

Frank obtained his driver's license in March 1937 and bought his first car, a 1929 Model A Ford Tudor. Then three years later on May 11, 1940, he made a major purchase for a used 1936 Black LaSalle 2 door Trigon Sedan. His trade in for the Ford was $40.00 and with $260.00 cash bought the LaSalle. The LaSalle was a heavy car around 3,060 pounds and had an eight-cylinder inline engine. A new 1936 LaSalle sold for $1,200. What a delight this car must have been.

Figure 22 1936 Black LaSalle

I was five years old then, and I can remember getting in the back seat when Frank took it out for a test drive. One day he was on his way to work when, without knowing, he backed the car into mom's clothesline. The handle on the rear trunk caught the clothesline and Frank dragged the clothesline, clothes and all right into downtown Le Roy when the locals were struck with awe. I'm sure he got quite a kidding from friends and a scolding from mom. Frank must have been saving his money since one day he bought a play pedal car for the author. What a pleasant surprise that was. One day he went to a farm auction and bought a horsehide for himself. Mom questioned what it was for, but she never did get an answer.

Figure 23 Billy and His Pedal Car

Frank continued his dream of aeronautics by enrolling in Aeronautical Engineering at the International Correspondence Schools at Scranton, PA, on August 25, 1937. Tuition was $220.00, which was discounted to $176.00 for paying cash. Remember this was the middle of the Great Depression so it appears Frank saved very well. In 1936, the median family income was $1,160 per year, so this represents at least 15% of his annual income. Frank pursued this educational course well into 1942 when he was serving in the Army.

The war in Europe was progressing rapidly by 1939 with Germany's invasion of Poland. The citizens of America wanted to pursue a hands-off or isolationist policy, but the war clouds were growing, and President Roosevelt was secretly taking measures to prepare for WWII. In response to the Selective Service Proclamation of the President of the United States, Frank registered for Selective Service on October 16, 1940. Just six months later on April 22, 1941, Frank was classed as IA, which immediately made him eligible for the draft. His order by the local board in Le Roy was number 497. Only one month later, in May 1941, he received his notice to report for duty at the Niagara Falls, Fort Niagara Army Induction Center. There was practically no time to enlist, which would have been much better for him since he would have been given a better chance for serving in a branch of service other than the infantry.

Proverbs 1:8-9, "Listen my son to your father's instruction and do not forsake your mother's teaching. They will be a garland to grace your head and a chain to adorn your neck."

"****"

Chapter Four

Induction
May to June 1941

On May 15, 1941, Frank reported to the Army Induction Station in Buffalo, N.Y., where he was given a physical exam to determine fitness for duty. His induction papers show his trade as a sheet metal worker with a weekly wage of $22, which is 55 cents per hour or an annual amount of $1,144. Indeed not much money, but in the Great Depression, he was fortunate to have a job at all. His vision was 20/30 in both eyes and a blood pressure of 130 over 80. He was indeed a healthy almost 24-year-old. He was rated A-1, "Mentally and physically qualified for the active military service of the United States."

At about this time his brother Al, who was 20 at the time, was rated as 4F, that is, not qualified for military service. After the draft was instituted in 1940, not all young men who registered, were accepted into the service. Thirty percent of registrants across America were rejected for physical defects. The 4-F classification was given primarily for muscular and bone malformations, hearing or circulatory ailments, mental deficiency or disease. On the same day as his physical, Frank reported for duty at the Fort Niagara Induction Center near Youngstown, NY. The center was at the site of Old Fort Niagara, which is located where the Niagara River, carrying water from Lake Erie, passing over Niagara Falls, flows to Lake Ontario. After two weeks, the family visited on May 30th, Decoration Day, traveling from Le Roy, N.Y., which is only about 60 miles away. Frank had sent a map showing the location and details on where to contact him.

Figure 24 Map for Fort Niagara Visitors

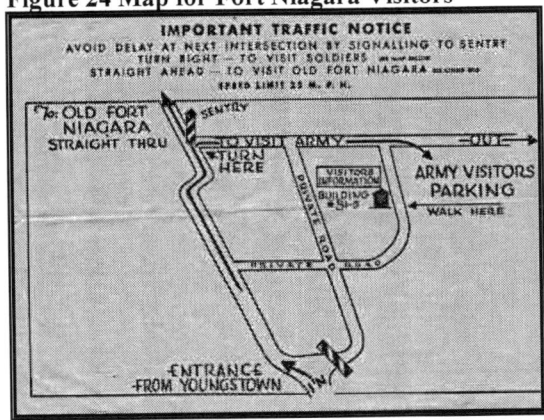

That visit must have been a joyous one, especially spending time with Frank in his smart Army uniform. Note the formal dress worn by the family, which was normal for holidays and Sunday church. The author was only five at the time, and I was very excited about seeing Frank. Family visiting included sister Eleanor and Mannie Costa, who were engaged at the time, sister Mary, and brother Al, cousin Ann Longhany, and Aunt Mary Brown.

Figure 25 Frank, Mom, Mary, Dad, Al & Billy

Since I was only five at the time, I have some difficulty remembering details about Frank. I do remember him buying me toys and playing around with me. The picture above shows the warm relationship we had. There was an age difference of 18 years since Frank was the first-born and I was the last born in the family. His time at Ft. Niagara was only three weeks. He writes in his diary that he went to Mass in the morning on Decoration Day, May 30th, and in the afternoon, the family came to see him.

Figure 26 Frank & Billy

He got a pass to go home on Saturday, June 1, 1941, and viewed his 8 mm color movie that he recently filmed. He left for Fort. Niagara at 7 and got there at 10:30 PM on Sunday.

Frank faithfully made entries in the army diary from May 14, 1941, to March 29, 1942. He started with the following: Serial No. 32131532, 5 feet, 10.5 inches tall, 160 pounds and 23 years old.

Figure 27 Frank's Diary

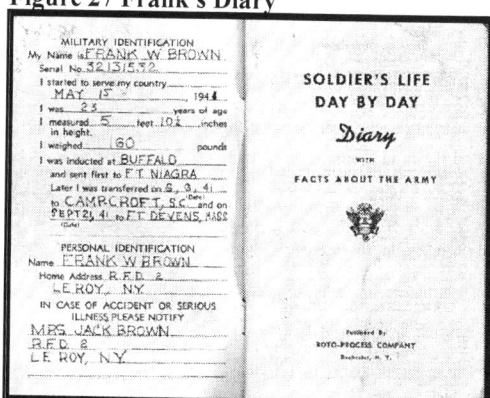

A timeline of Frank's military service, starting at the Fort Niagara Induction Center, is provided in Appendix A and is portrayed in detail in the chapters ahead.

Proverbs 3:5-6, "Trust in the Lord with all your heart and lean not on your own understanding; in all your ways acknowledge him, and he will make your paths straight.

"*****"

Chapter Five

Camp Croft
June to September 1941

On June 7, 1941, Frank left Ft. Niagara and traveled by Erie Railroad through PA, MD, VA, DC, N.C. and S.C. He was fortunate to have a Pullman upper berth, which was a luxury to what lie ahead. As the train traveled through the south, Frank was surprised to see cabins with chinked mud, not seen up north. After a 26-hour trip, he arrived at Camp Croft on June 8th, which is a few miles from Spartanburg, SC. Camp Croft was a new training camp with the capacity to house and train 15,000 men.

Figure 28 Camp Croft 1941

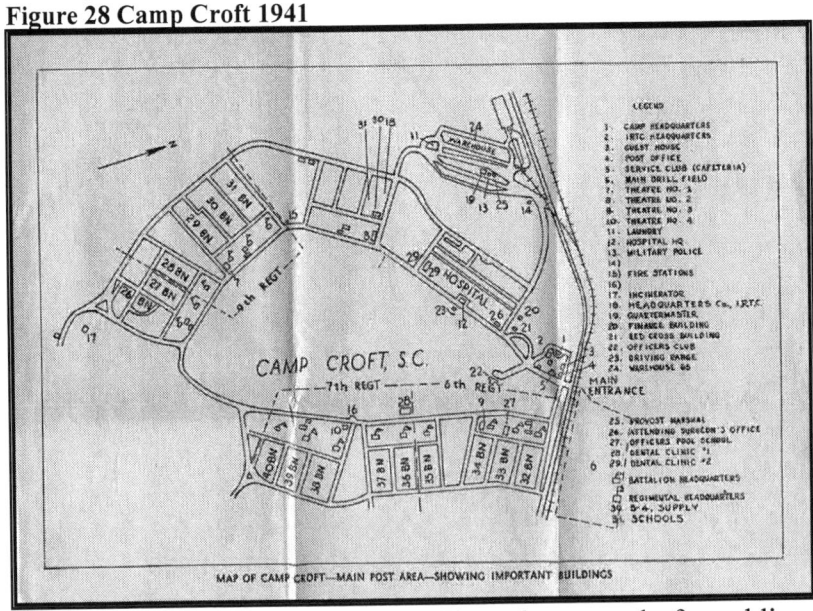

The camp was started December 5, 1940, and was ready for soldiers by May 1941. This link describes Camp Croft in 1941: http://www.schistory.net/campcroft/index.html. The training started

30

out very rough during the first two weeks at camp. Here are a few entries from his diary.

June 10th Tuesday - We were reclassified. Drilled all day, very warm. Joe Wahl had sunstroke.

June 11th Wednesday - Two more went to the hospital this morning. Drilled all morning. Had more rest periods. Moved today to new barracks. Assigned to Co. C, 30th Infantry, Training Battalion. Drilled today. Started to learn the manual of arms. Started to rain heavily.

June 12th Thursday - Had relay race competition. 4th platoon took 1st place twice.

June 13th Friday - Was busy all night getting ready for inspection in the morning. Finally got some mail, four letters.

June 14th Saturday - Rained a little in the afternoon. Went to Canteen, got soap for laundry.

June 15th Sunday - Went to mass & communion. Wrote letter. Went for a walk at nite & enjoyed it very much.

June 16th Monday - Started our first week of our 13 week training period. Learned how to pitch a tent.

June 17th Tuesday - Was on fatigue detail in the afternoon. No mail.

June 18th Wednesday - Was on KP (Kitchen Police) today. Never worked harder on KP. Didn't get through until 8 pm. Signed payroll. Camera arrived from home.

June 19th Thursday - Got my field equipment. Learned to make a full field pack. Sent out laundry. Wrote letter home.

June 20th Friday - Dug first foxhole (what a job) on my back. Pitched tents in the afternoon.

Frank received training on first aid, sanitation, use of a compass and how to recognize mustard gas. He appreciated the watch that his brother Al had given him as a going away present, and used it to prepare for hearing the sergeant blowing his whistle for assembly. The barracks were new and equipped with good cots. He was issued blue denim overalls and told not to wear the blue O.D. hat since prisoners in South Carolina wear them. On June 20th, the first foxholes had to be dug on their backs with their small pack shovel. The hole had to be 7 feet deep with length and width of the body. After pitching tents, four companies, 800 men, did a five-mile march with full packs, which included gas masks, web belts with first aid and canteens. Later the training would extend marching to 25 miles.

Frank would get letters from mom about every two or three days. Less frequently he would receive letters from his sisters Mary or Eleanor, brother Al, Aunt Fran, Katie, Elizabeth, and Mary. Packages would arrive with cookies, chocolates, various candies and many times would include a $1 or $5 bill, which sure would help since the army pay was very low. Sometimes he would receive chocolates from the Jell-O Company where he worked before entering service.

He was issued a new Garand M1 rifle and instructed on how to assemble, disassemble and keep it oiled and clean.

Figure 29 Frank with M-1 Garand Rifle

The army was very strict on keeping your weapons clean as Frank soon found out and it would take up to two hours to clean a rifle to pass inspection. You could not have one speck of dirt or rust showing.

Soon the routine at Camp Croft became about the same each day as follows:

5:00 am, reveille, wash, dress, fall out in formation, clean barracks.
6:15 am, eat breakfast, clean barracks.
7:15 - 7:45 am, physical training.
8:00 - 8:50 am, drill.
9:00 - 9:50 am, training with weapons.
10:00 - 11:45 am, special training.
12:00 - 1:00 pm, lunch.
1:00 - 4:30 pm, instruction on weapons.
5:30 pm, dinner.
9:00 pm, bedtime for Frank.
11:00 pm, lights out.

On July 1, 1941, Frank received bayonet practice and made the remark in a letter home, *"I hope we never have to use them."*

Figure 30 Bayonet Practice

He then proceeded to the firing range and fired 18 rounds with the Springfield bolt-action rifle with a score of two bulls eyes and eight in the #4 circle. Also, he fired the Garand M-1 rifle, which holds eight rounds that fire each time you squeeze the trigger. Some think that it fires all eight rounds by holding the trigger down, but this is not true. Frank writes that it has the same kick as a 12-gauge shotgun. At the 84 ft. range he got one bulls eye and seven in the outer circle. Frank's buddy missed the target entirely but managed to hit the wheels on the trolley that tows the targets! What a sad beginning. Marksmanship was only the start of many months of training on the range where they would fire for record.

The week of July 6, 1941, there were more weapons training with the Browning machine gun.

Figure 31 Frank & Buddy on Machine Gun Drill

Frank then fired the 45-caliber revolver and after firing 20 rounds, he made only 72 out of 200, which was not a good score. As I discovered later when I

33

participated in USAF basic training, target shooting with a 45 is very challenging. Truth being, the first time firing, I shot the legs off the wooden stand holding the target. No score!

This is one of many cartoons that Frank drew and placed in his letters written to his mom. They usually portrayed his younger brother Billy at home or in army situations. The collection is shown in Appendix B.

Frank made several friends after only a few short weeks in camp. From the New York State area, there was LeBaron (Buffalo), John Dubois (Buffalo), Barber (Bergen), Elholm (Buffalo), Bailey (Cuylerville), Jim Foyster (Buffalo), Chenez (Lockport), Knoll (Lancaster) and Santangelo (Rochester). Friends from home were a pleasure, but home seemed so far away. About this time Frank learned that his sister Mary had Undulant fever, caused by milk from a sick cow from the local Johnson farm. The milk was unpasteurized, so it carried the bacteria causing Undulant fever or Brucellosis. She suffered from fever and joint pain, and the only cure was to wait it out. Frank was concerned so far from home and wrote that she should get treatments, but there were none.

On July 5, 1941, Frank's brother Billy had a close call with a car in the home driveway. Louise Maher, a relative of the family, was learning how to drive with her husband, Ray. They made a trip down from Buffalo, and when turning into the driveway on Warsaw Road, she lost control and headed for Billy on his Red Ryder wagon in front of the back door. Billy saw the car coming and ran for his life, but his Red Ryder was hit broadside. After the excitement was over, Louise said they would buy Billy a new wagon, but that never happened. Billy's dad banged out the damage and the Red Ryder was back in action. Frank was relieved to know that the only casualty was the prized wagon.

Vic Regone, Frank's cousin who was also in service, sent a letter to Frank that he got home on a three-day pass on July 4, 1941 since he was being transferred from Mitchell Field on Long Island to Iceland. They were issued fur-lined coats, skis and boots and were leaving soon. Vic had enlisted the same time as Frank and due to his radio experience was assigned to the First Division in communications.

Guard duty was new for Frank but would become routine over the next few years. He wrote on July 15, 1941, that he was on guard duty that night starting at 6:00 PM, walked the post for two hours, rested 4 hours, back at 12:00 AM and repeated the sequence to 6:00 AM. He carried a 45 automatic, unloaded, and a club. He would try doors to supply rooms and mess halls and challenge persons when necessary and when challenged would have to halt and identify themselves. That night he challenged an Officer of the Day and a sergeant in a car. Not a very eventful night.

On July 21, 1941, all the men listened to Presidents Roosevelt's speech to the nation. The President said men would be discharged 28 years and over if Congress passes the bill. Frank remarks in his diary, *"I'm afraid I will be in for more than one year now if they let them out."* After the December attack on Pearl Harbor, all of this would change and those men discharged and in the reserve would be recalled. Frank at this time was 24 so was not eligible.

During the time at Camp Croft, Frank would go into Spartanburg on weekends usually with John Dubois from Buffalo, and enjoy a movie, southern fried chicken dinner and one or two sundaes. While in Spartanburg Frank found a unique toy for Billy that he sent home to surprise him. The toy was a ceramic statue of a little boy eating a watermelon under a cotton tree.

Figure 32 Toy Frank Sent Billy

Frank continued to receive packages from home with cookies, fudge, and candy. The Jell-O Company would send candy as well, and this certainly helped to keep up the morale of Frank and others. Of course, when a

35

soldier got a package of goodies, he would pass it around so all could share in the pleasure. After all, there was no way a soldier could hide his goodies from 30 men in an open barracks.

Another routine a soldier had to experience was barrack's inspection, sometimes twice a day. On August 7, 1941, it was a sad day for the platoon when they failed barracks inspection twice. Instructions were very clear that every bed has to be made with no wrinkles in the blankets. Dust must be wiped off everything, windows sparkling clean, no ashes in the heating stove, lavatories clean and, of course, uniform and locker in top notch condition. Sometimes the Colonel would do the inspection much to their surprise.

The physical training exercises became more frequent and more demanding. Every morning they ran the obstacle course which included the low and high hurdle, 7 and 10 ft smooth wall, climb under two logs set 2 ft from the ground, jump a ditch 6 ft across, and do a balanced run of narrow board 10 inches wide and zigzag for 20 ft. Next were five low hurdles on a run and jump a creek, and finally run through several tires on the ground. On August 7, 1941, two men sprained ankles on the creek jump, so the Colonel closed the course. Frank writes, *"We were just learning to jump the creek with rifles but will not get a chance now. I really liked this course. It was more fun than on the athletic field going through monotonous exercises. Time to go to Post Exchange for ice cream."* Frank sure would put an optimistic spin on the most difficult.

On August 8th, Frank encountered an incident at the mess hall during breakfast. He writes, *"We regularly go to the mess hall for breakfast and stand by the table. When everyone is in, mess sergeant blows a whistle and then we can sit down and eat. This morning we waited by our tables about 3 to 4 minutes and no whistle. Then a sergeant said there was too much noise, and we would stand a while longer. That was the straw that broke the camel's back. About 40 of us walked right out of the mess hall. When we got to our barracks, the First Sergeant blew his whistle, and we lined up in the street. He asked what was the trouble. Not one of us answered. He said we should not have walked out but he realized we had to stand too long sometimes, so he marched us back, told mess sergeant from now on we can sit down and eat as soon as we come in and as long as we are quiet."* What a good ending to what could have been discipline. Frank showed spunk in this incident and a sign of courage in standing for what he thought was unfair treatment. However, when you are in the Army you no longer have the freedom to judge and seek fair treatment. I'm sure Frank learned the difference very soon, and it showed in his receiving good marks and promotions.

Frank and his buddies were trained on firing 81 mm mortars on August 15th after a five-mile march to the firing range and then five miles back to camp.

Figure 33 Mortar Practice

On the way, they passed through a town and a small boy about four years old saluted as they passed. That sure helped the morale of the men. Frank had his camera and took a swell picture of the boy. It reminded him of his brother Billy back home, who would likely do the same thing.

Figure 34 Young Boy Saluting Soldiers

They ate dinner in the field with a mess kit, which consisted of spoon, knife, fork, cup and pan. There was a beautiful peach orchard on the range full of ripe Lucifer peaches. They ate until they couldn't look at another peach again. He writes, *"The peaches are the finest I have ever tasted."*

Figure 35 Frank Eating Lucifer Peaches

That night Frank went to a show put on by Camel cigarettes and said it wasn't very good. The cigarette companies would push the sale of tobacco in those days, and the cost of a pack was dirt-cheap. Little did anyone know how much harm the tobacco was causing until later in life. Now playing jokes on your fellow bedmates were common, so Frank did one on Barber that night by putting a squeegee in his bed and turned Bailey's bed around and jacked it up. I'm sure Frank got paid back soon.

On August 18th, Frank learned that Congress passed the 2 1/2 year training bill by a vote of 203 to 202, which stated men would now train for at least this length of time. Frank wrote, *"It doesn't discourage me one bit. When I entered the army, I had a pretty good idea that I would be in for more than a year. I won't mind it if I can get home once in a while. We have only about four more weeks here. When I get to my next post, I probably will be able to get a ten-day furlough."* Time would later show how hard it would be to get a furlough. Frank did know that since he was stationed about 800 miles from home, it would take at least a 10-day furlough to make it practical. That day Frank found out that two hometown friends, Tommy Ryan and Gerald Schaunesey, were stationed three miles from camp. He made a surprise visit, and it was a pleasant surprise to all and boosted their spirits.

The next day Frank had his turn at KP (kitchen police). KP duty was a detail in the Mess Hall where you had to do whatever the cook told you to do. It could be preparing vegetables, dishwashing, and pot scrubbing, sweeping and mopping floors, wiping tables, and serving food on the chow line. Frank said he never did like washing dishes but had no choice in the army. Frank took this photo of buddies on KP peeling potatoes. Many times KP was given as a punishment for minor infractions a soldier might commit.

Figure 36 Time for KP

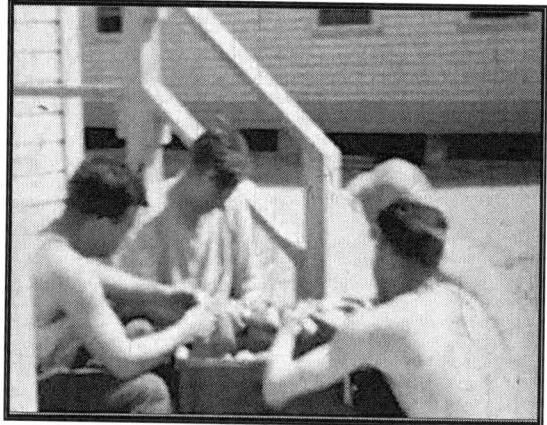

At the end of August 1941, Frank wrote that several men were putting in for a four-day furlough over the Labor Day holiday. Oliver Barber and Frank thought about going home but did not request it since going, and coming takes about two days, leaving only two days at home. Frank says in his diary, *"Hard decision to make. Am completely broke."* However, Frank was to get a lockjaw (tetanus) shot on Wednesday, and the round-trip train fare was $24, which he did not have. He was eligible for 30 days leave a year so thought it best to wait until the next camp assignment. Then on September 3, it was made known that six men from Frank's platoon had not returned yet. If they were not back in three days, they would face disciplinary action. Five men from another platoon went AWOL (Absent Without Leave), hired a taxi and got in an accident on the way home. One was killed, and four were injured. Those injured would have to pay their hospital bills and then serve time when they return. Discipline is not easy in the army but necessary.

On the weekends, it was normal practice to get a ride to the nearest town, which was Spartanburg. On August 31st, Frank, Dubois, Barber, Bailey, and Alexander went to a recreation hall in Spartanburg. They played a few games of shuffleboard and basketball. After that, they were persuaded to sing and got quite a few laughs since none could carry a tune in a basket, but they had plenty of fun. The next day Frank and Dubois set out to hitchhike to Greenville, SC, but could not get a ride so they went to Spartanburg again. They had two sodas each and were sitting on a park bench when an elderly woman drove up and asked them if they would like a ride to Rainbow Lake. They jumped at the chance and on the way she picked up three more soldiers. Rainbow Lake wasn't much of a lake, but they stayed about an hour and then the woman drove them around and showed them the sites in Spartanburg. Now stop for a minute and think about that happening in today's world. That woman deserves a medal for this remarkable act of kindness to our military. Being so far from home it sure would make a soldier feel good.

On September 8, 1941, Frank completed 12 weeks of basic training, and he was sure glad that it was over. September 10th, Frank was offered a promotion to corporal if he would train new recruits in Missouri. He turned it down since he thought it would be too far from home and wanted to get home soon to see the folks. There was a farewell dinner with singing and speeches on September 11th, and John Dubois was a hit, being a natural born comedian. They heard President Roosevelt's speech on the radio and it sounded like the war was close at hand. On September 16th, Frank writes in his diary, *"Ollie (Barber) and John (Dubois) left for home at 5 pm. I had a hard time keeping a stiff upper lip. I will miss them as will anyone who has known them as I. Barrack is beginning to look empty."* Barber and DuBois were being discharged since they were over the age of 28. Frank was notified on September 18th that he was being transferred to Ft Devens, about 38 miles northwest of Boston. All the men of Company C were being moved to different locations for specialized training. On September 19th, Frank left for Ft Devens at 7:20 PM.

Proverbs 1:7, "The fear of the Lord is the beginning of knowledge, but fools despise wisdom and discipline."

"*****"

Chapter Six

Fort Devens to Dix to Benning
September to December 1941

Frank arrived at Ft. Devens on September 21, 1941, around 5 am after passing through Washington, Philly, Trenton, Newark and Jersey City. The soldiers were examined in the cold morning air and then separated. Frank was assigned to the 16th Infantry radio school to learn code and the operation of the new walkie-talkie set.

Figure 37 Walkie Talkie

The walkie-talkie was formerly called the handie talkie or SCR-536. It went into mass production in early 1941 and was the first handheld two-way radio developed in 1940 by Galvin Manufacturing, now Motorola.

Frank was still hoping to get a furlough but was told no on September 25th and was very disappointed. On the next day, he took the code aptitude test and got the second highest mark in the group and then on September 30th started radio school including the operation of the walkie-talkie sets. For some unknown reason, a truck driving test came about, but he failed since he couldn't double clutch properly. In just over two weeks, on October 6, 1941, he finished training and left Ft. Devens, MA, by convoy at 9:10 pm. They arrived at Ft. Dix, N.J., at 7:30 am and he was immediately assigned to the 12 Infantry, 1st Battalion, Company C, 2nd Platoon, 1st Squad, where he would remain for the remainder of his military service. He now slept in a tent with five cots and a stove. The tent leaked, and they issued him a 1903 rifle, a real antique. So this was the Army, Mr. Brown!

Three days later on October 9th, back home, Dad went to clean the chimney since winter was soon approaching and in those days, you would take a flashlight battery, break it open, light the carbon and drop it down the chimney to burn out the creosote. Strange as this may sound, apparently it worked. It was around the noon hour, and the roof was wet from the rain. He used an extension ladder to reach the roof and carried up a stepladder to prop against the chimney. When he got on the stepladder, it slipped, and he fell to the ground just missing the concrete rainwater tank by a few inches. The stepladder came down behind him and struck him in the back. Mom called the ambulance, and he was taken to St. Jerome hospital in Batavia, N.Y., in critical condition. Mom apparently did not want to alarm Frank so far from home, so she only wrote that he had a fall. Then five days later on October 13th and 14th he received a total of three letters saying that Dad was in the hospital. Frank writes back, *"I was surprised to hear Dad is in the hospital. I had a feeling something was wrong. Tell him to take care of himself and do just as the doctor's say. He shouldn't get up until the doctors say that he can."* Frank did not know his condition was critical but sensed that something was wrong, so he tried to get an emergency furlough. The problem was a blood clot had formed in his Dad's leg, and there was a possibility that if the clot went to his heart, it would kill him. At this time, Frank was told by the First Sergeant that all men who failed to make a qualifying score with the rifle needn't expect furloughs or passes. You can be sure that was reason enough to improve his rifle score.

October 18th, Frank got a four-day pass to go home because of the family emergency. He left Ft. Dix, N.J., at 1 pm, got a bus from Trenton to Newark and from Newark to Batavia, arriving home at 5 am Sunday. He notes in his diary that he surprised everyone and found Dad to be very sick. On Sunday, after Frank arrived, Dad went home against the doctor's orders. After being home only 10 hours, Frank left at 3 pm on a train for New York City and then took a Philly bus to Bordentown and arrived at Ft. Dix 4:30 am, noting that the trip only cost him $17.20. Upon returning, he was so worried about Dad that he phoned Mrs. Meehan, a neighbor across the street, from a phone booth at the Post Exchange (PX). There was some difficulty in making the call and when connecting there was so much noise at the PX he could barely hear. On top of that, some goon was pounding on the booth shouting he was taking too long. Frank gave him a piece of his mind and the person on the phone wondered just what was going on. Finally, Mrs. Meehan told Frank that Dad was doing better and not to worry.

Two days later, Wednesday, October 22nd, he was immediately ordered to pack bags and prepare for a trip to Ft. Benning on a truck convoy. That trip took three days and was very tiring. On the way, he rode in a command car to Camp Lee, VA, and then slept on the ground after supper at 9 pm. He was up a 3:30 am, rode all day and passed his future Camp Gordon near Augusta, GA.

Figure 38 Ft Benning (Columbus) to Ft Gordon (Augusta)

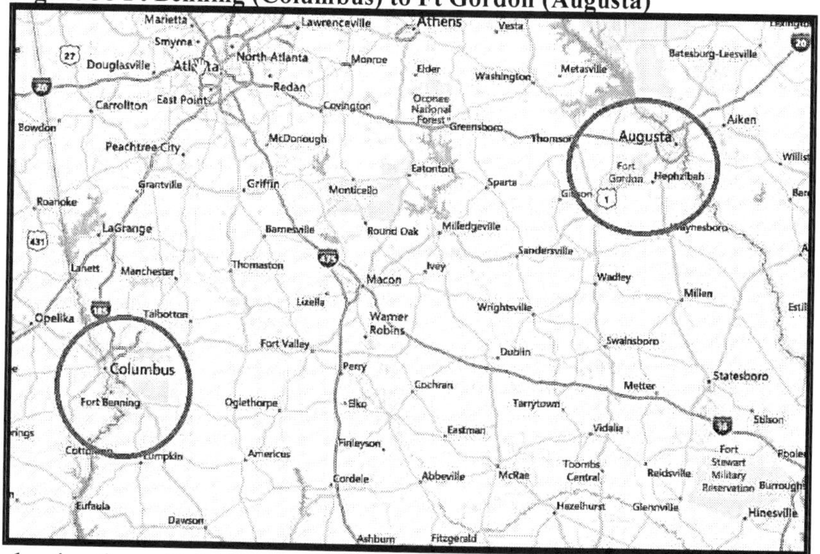

His destination, Ft. Benning, is near Columbus, GA, and was a temporary camp for the 12th Infantry, since Camp Gordon near Augusta, was a new camp and not ready yet. Frank was assigned to the Fourth Motorized Division, 12th Infantry Regiment. The Fourth Division, one of the oldest in the army, was known by the Cloverleaf insignia and had previously fought in the Civil War, Spanish American War and WWI. At about this time the Fourth Division was near full strength and the firepower was increased to achieve the army's first motorized division, which was a new concept. However, two years later, due to unknown reasons, it was changed to primarily an infantry division. Regiment strength at this time was 91 officers and 2,641 men including 56 of the Medical Detachment. At this time, orders were received to discharge and transfer to the Enlisted Reserve Corps 100 men over 28 years of age per the law recently passed by Congress. (1)

When Frank arrived at Ft. Benning, he wrote a letter home telling mom that his brother Al should quit vocational school and get a job to help support the family since it appeared that dad would be out of work for some time. At the same time, Frank's sister Eleanor was getting married on October 25th, which had been planned for months. Dad could not attend the wedding since he was bed ridden due to the blood clot in his leg. Frank told them to use savings in his bank account to help buy food and pay expenses. I'm sure Frank felt somewhat helpless being confined so far from home and with communications limited to letters. He was not a worry type person and was in fact very positive in his daily thoughts regardless of his circumstances. However as it turned out Dad's healing process would indeed be very slow and the months ahead would be very trying to the entire family.

Figure 39 Postcard from Ashtabula Ohio

His sister Eleanor was married to Mannie (Dominic) Costa on October 25, 1941, and they took a week of a honeymoon to Chicago where they stayed with Eleanor's Uncle Bill and Aunt Frances. She wrote several postcards home every day on their trip by auto, staying in tourist homes, seeing beautiful Lake Erie and then the big city of Chicago.

In Chicago, there were shopping, trains and taxies and seeing a radio show called Plantation Party at the Merchandise Mart. Then Aunt Fran bought the couple silverware service for 12, which was a very gracious gift. It was good to receive good news from home on Mannie and Eleanor's marriage and to see life go on despite the winds of war on the horizon. That week, Frank wrote home again

Figure 40 Postcard to Billy from Sister Eleanor

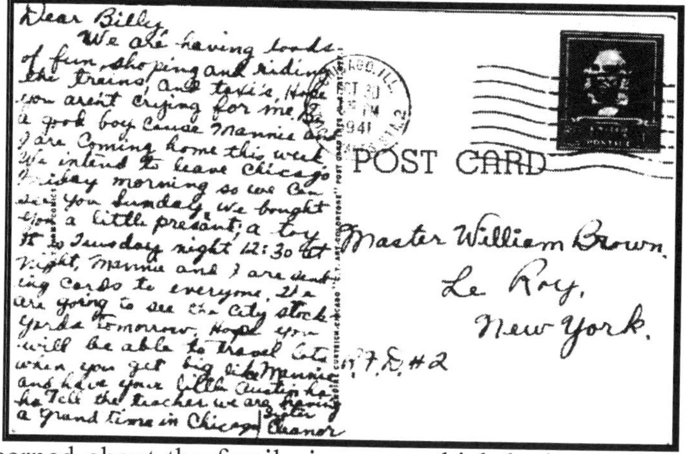
Dear Billy
We are having loads
of fun shoping and riding
the trains and taxi's. Hope
you aren't crying for me. Be
a good boy cause Mannie and
I are coming home this week
We intend to leave Chicago
Friday morning so we can
see you Sunday. We bought
you a little present; a toy
It is Tuesday night 12:30 at
night, Mannie and I are sending cards to everyone. We
are going to see the city stock
yards tomorrow. Hope you
will be able to travel lots
when you get big like Mannie
and have your little Austin ha
ha Tell the teacher we are having
a grand time in Chicago
Sister
Eleanor

POST CARD

Master William Brown
Le Roy,
New York.
R.F.D. #2

concerned about the family income, which had ceased since Dad's confinement. He instructed mom again to draw from his small savings account at the local bank.

On October 30th, Frank went on maneuvers for three weeks starting with a bivouac in the woods at Thompson, GA. Next day they arrived at a forest near Richburg, S.C., and skipped pitching tents until 2 am when it started to rain. Hurriedly the tent got pitched in a downpour. On Sunday, he caught a ride to Chester, S.C., and went to church, bought stamps, and walked all the way back to camp, about 12 miles. He inquired about a dependency discharge, but there would be no consideration until maneuvers were over. During the next three weeks, they camped 25 miles north of Columbia, Jinkinsville, Lancaster, and Pageland S.C. There were daily war games between the Reds, Frank's group and the Blues. One day did not go so well when the company commander and his first sergeant were captured. Of course, there were the complaints that the umpires were prejudiced against the Reds and the Blues thought the same. On November 7, 1941, Frank and the Reds were quite startled when the cavalry (that's right, men on horseback) rode straight through their camp. The cavalry, being the Blues, were confused and thought the Reds were Blues and to their surprise were captured. However since they were on rations for a few days, it may have been intentional since they were quite hungry for real food. So much for war games! November 10th, Frank was on guard duty all day and that night they were in a blackout. It was cold sleeping on the ground, which was the norm for the next several days. On the 14th he was on guard duty again, missed supper and had only bread and slice of cheese, so he went to the canteen and bought cookies and candy. By the 15th he was feeling quite dirty not having a bath for several days, so he took a bath in a creek ignoring the frigid water.

The battle of Reds against the Blues continued on for several days and on the 17th, the Reds were successful with the aid of tanks. However, he was on guard duty on a riverbank all night with no relief, no sleep and little food. On the 19th, they found themselves surrounded, so around 5 pm they bivouacked near a farmhouse where he got his first drink of water in 24 hours. He slept well that night but on the next day, they fought the Blues 44th Division all day and lost most all engagements. The Reds believed the umpires were unfair and were ready to take revenge. So at sunrise, the 12th ran their trucks straight through the Blue forces. Frank thought there would have been many casualties in a real war. They drove all morning until they reached the 4th Division again. On Sunday, the 23rd, it was indeed a good day since they got Thanksgiving dinner in the field after which he had a chance to see the town of Lancaster. The next night they rode a convoy in a blackout with the half-tracs only seeing the red tail lights of the half-tracs in front of them. Frank had a good time manning the machine gun sitting high on the vehicle. Finally on the 28th, the maneuvers ended at 5 pm, so Frank went to a basketball game with Al MacDonald "Mac" and Birmingham, which they enjoyed very much. On November 29th, since the maneuvers were over and they were just 10 miles from Chester, SC, Frank and Mac got permission to hike to Camp Croft, which was 50 miles away. They thought it would be a good time to say good-bye to some friends before leaving for the new Camp Gordon in Georgia. They started out 6:30 pm and arrived at Camp Croft at 11:00 pm. The first thing they did was get a hot shower, which was the first since leaving Camp Croft three weeks ago. Frank writes home, *"It was sure nice sleeping in a cot for a change. This afternoon we had a swell dinner, and we actually ate off of*

plates and then we went to a movie. We made good time getting back to the regiment." We can certainly see what was motivating these two to make that 50-mile journey hitchhiking. No doubt it was more than just saying goodbye to camp friends. That shower and real food must have been delightful!

The next few days at Chester were spent preparing for the convoy trip to Ft. Benning near Columbus, GA since they were informed Camp Gordon would not be ready for another three weeks. On December 2, 1941, Frank was phone orderly and caught particular hell for leaving the phone to find a Lieutenant. In the interim, there was not much news from home on Dad getting any better. Frank wrote, *"Why do you have to take Dad's temperature twice a day and why does he have to stay off his legs? Is he getting any better?"* On December 5th, they left by convoy for Ft. Benning and bivouacked at Thompson, GA, a few miles west of Augusta. The next day they continued and made Ft. Benning where they would remain living in tents for three weeks until they could move to their permanent base at Camp Gordon.

On December 6th, they were notified that if they wanted a furlough by Christmas, they would have to buy their railroad or bus tickets ahead of time. Frank and others went to Columbus, GA and he purchased a railroad round trip ticket for $26.70. The next morning December 7th, he was told that his furlough was approved for December 13th to 28th, but then in the afternoon, they got the shocking news of the Japanese attack on Pearl Harbor. Frank wrote, *"Our furloughs now are likely canceled. What a fine Christmas present."* The next day, December 8th, Congress declared war on Japan and Frank writes, *"Don't worry. No sense in borrowing trouble."* He sure had a positive attitude in the face of now declared war and the high possibility of not getting home for some time.

On December 13th, they drew lots for furloughs again, but he drew an X again. He writes in his diary, *"I drew wrong slip- Couldn't go. Felt bad. Went to town. Sent telegram home. Bought Billy a toy. Sent it home."* Now due to war, only one-fourth of the company can be absent at one time so in his squad 10 out of 14 can't go home. However, he was issued a new Garand M-1 rifle replacing the old one that was so hard to clean. Next chance for furlough would be December 29th, but he was not too confident on that either. On the 19th, he received a package of candy and cookies from home and several letters from cousins and aunts; that sure made him feel much better. On the 20th, he writes in his diary, *"I was a prison guard again and three prisoners to guard with only two rounds of ammo in my gun."* Frank had a sense of humor even in the worst of times.

He sent home some gifts for Christmas and had quite a laugh when he learned that Billy got a good bump on his head sledding down hill. Frank had not seen snow for a year and wondered what it was like in the cold and snow again. He had only thoughts of Christmas at home now and wrote, *"Hope Billy gets that toy chicken that lays eggs when you crank it. Received box candy and cookies."*

At this time, Frank applied for National Service Life Insurance in the amount of $5,000 with the principal beneficiary named as his mother. The National Life Insurance Act of 1940 allowed servicemen to purchase life insurance without a physical examination. The $5,000 policy cost $3.35 per month, which was withdrawn from his pay.

On December 21st, he got up at 3 am and left Ft. Benning at 6 am in a convoy of trucks. It was goodbye to Benning and hello to Ft. Gordon near Augusta, GA. They arrived at 4 pm and unloaded several railroad boxcars and trucks.

Psalm 73:28, "As for me, it is good to be near God. I have made the Sovereign Lord my refuge; I will tell of all your deeds."

"****"

Chapter Seven

Camp Gordon
December 1941 to July 1942

Camp Gordon was larger than Ft. Benning and had many more amenities. Frank wrote in his diary December 22, 1941, *"No lights or water in barracks yet, but now we have plates to eat on. First time since leaving Ft. Devens."* A few days later on Christmas Eve, the company drew lots for furloughs while Frank was at HQ on runner duty, so he didn't get a chance to draw. He notes in his diary, *"Can't get home for New Years. Disappointed so went to midnight mass. Ate some of mother's fruit cake before going to bed."* Frank questioned the First Sergeant about when he could get a furlough, and the sergeant became angry at the request to where Frank became too angry to argue. Later he found out that the company commander was gone, and the First Sergeant was completely overwhelmed with work since he was in charge of the recent move to Camp Gordon.

The soldiers of the 12th Regiment were treated quite well to a Christmas feast on December 25th consisting of roast turkey, corn, peas, olives, salad, sweet and mashed potatoes, rolls and pumpkin pie with ice cream. Afterward, they sang songs and had a good time although there were many with thoughts of Christmas and their loved ones back home, which seemed so far away.

Figure 41 Frank's Portrait

An artist in Battalion 1 drew an excellent portrait of Frank on January 1st, which he later sent home for Dad and Mom. On January 5th, Frank heard from home that Dad's X-Rays showed good results and the toy he had sent Billy did not work, but he liked it just the same. On the same day, he drew again for a furlough with number 50, but only numbers 1 through 43 could go on January 12th. He wrote in his diary, *"Drew lots for furloughs. Lost again. Seem to have no end of bad luck. Won't get a furlough for a long time now."* He got good news from home, however, that Dad could return to work on a new job, which would help with the strained family finances. However, there was bad news that the draft board classed Al as 1A, which meant he could be drafted soon. Frank advised his brother that he should volunteer for service in the Army to learn a trade that he could use after serving. Frank wrote his sister Mary on January 10, 1942, *"There isn't much recreation for soldiers on this post yet. You see they are still working on the theaters and probably won't have them finished for a month or two yet. If there is a library around here, I haven't found it. I buy a Saturday Evening Post every week, and that gives me something to read. Thursday night MacDonald and I went to a movie in Augusta and saw Belle Star. After the show, we both had a banana split and a sundae each. Next, we played three games of pool. I didn't know much about the game, so I lost the first two. After that, we ate a couple of hamburgers and went back to camp. All in all, we had a pretty good time."*

Figure 42 Frank's Camp Gordon Barracks

Then on January 12th, in his diary, he writes, *"Baker accidentally fired rifle inside barracks. The bullet went thru floor and locker upstairs. Luckily everyone outside for retreat. Went to town. Saw show."* He did not write home about that incident. Frank liked Camp Gordon since it was so close to Augusta, which was an advantage since the city was quite large and had many amenities.

Figure 43 Time at the Canteen

Camp Gordon in time had many facilities the other camps did not have. For example, there was the canteen where you could buy candy, the service club with many social affairs and the USO club where you could get sodas, milkshakes, sundaes and, of course, beer and other drinks.

Figure 44 Dance at the Recreation Hall

Dances were held with girls from Augusta with the regiment big band sound. There was the Post Exchange where you could buy many things at a good army price. Frank and his buddies would head for Augusta on weekends just to get away from the mess hall food and try some of that southern fried chicken cuisine. The barracks were, of course, very basic with no privacy unless you made sergeant and would bunk with a fellow sergeant in a corner room. Otherwise, you were in a row of bunks with a nighttime serenade in a varied frequency of snoring. There was a day room for reading and writing letters and

Figure 45 Mess Hall

the barracks were heated and had hot showers. All of this was a luxury as compared to tenting in the field.

Figure 46 Barracks Sleeping Arrangements

In January and February, the routine at the camp was the same as the other camps with morning calisthenics, drill, weapon instruction and rifle practice. Soon they would fire for record again. On January 13th, Frank, who previously was enrolled in Aeronautical Engineering with the International Correspondence School, decided to change the course for Sheet Metal as a trade. He thought that would be more practical for him when he would be discharged and back working at the Jell-O Company plant in his hometown, Le Roy, NY.

On the 21st, the movie theater and day room library opened up which had a pocket library. The base theater was large and played recent Hollywood movies every night. The only problem was the men were many times rambunctious, and you would have a hard time hearing the movie. This was no doubt the result of too many drinks at the serviceman's club. Frank was an avid reader of good literature and liked the classics, for example, the "Phantom Rickshaw" by Rudyard Kipling. He missed having a good well-stocked library. He bought Dale Carnegie's book, "How to Win

Figure 47 Camp Movie Theater

Friends, and Influence People" and enjoyed reading it in his spare time. On the 23rd, he was surprised to receive a $5.00 check from the Jell-O Company for a Christmas present.

Figure 48 Fourth Division Parade

The next day the Fourth Division had a parade for General Wallace, which was a prelude of many to come and were usually held on Saturday and Sunday. Many civilians would come from Augusta to view these parades of bands, soldiers and Army equipment putting on an impressive display. After a while, they became a little much as Frank would later write. The 12th Regiment also had a Drum and Bugle Corp, which Frank photographed at one of their events.

On January 18th, Sunday, the weather in Augusta was a mild 70 degrees F, so warm that people on the street were wearing their new outfits; almost like Easter. With the $5 Frank received from Jell-O Company and another $5 from Aunt Fran, Frank went to Augusta and bought a pair of OD wool trousers for $8.95. He said, *"They fit me much better in the waist than the Government Issue since the waist is 34 instead of 32 so I will wear these for dress only and the other for regular duty."* At this time, Frank applied for Officer

Figure 49 12th Regiment Drum & Bugle

Candidate School (OCS) and wrote, *"It's doubtful whether I will hear anything from it but there's no harm trying. If a man's application is accepted, he has to try an exam, and if he passes with a high mark, he can be sure he will be sent to OCS."* Then he added, *"I am in the pink of health. Yesterday I weighed myself and found that I tip the scales at 180 lbs. I guess I have put on a little weight this winter. How is Dad's leg coming along?"* A week later he found out that he was not selected for OCS since the company commander did not recommend him.

On a letter home dated February 11th, Frank described how busy he was and the time involved in taking care of your personal equipment. *"Today was rather a busy one for me. I was busy from reveille this morning till lights out tonight. After supper tonight I had to wash my web equipment, that is rifle belt, leggings and shovel cover. Then I had to pack an alert bag, my canvas bag, and my seat. The alert bag is the bag we take with us when we move. It contains extra clothing. The canvas bag carries extra under clothing and toilet articles. This bag has replaced the old pack, and it is worn on the back like the old pack. The seat is my seat on the half-trac. It has a zipper and when packed contains the extra blankets which go to make it a good cushion when we go riding. We are going on a practice run tomorrow, and that is why we had to get all packed tonight."*

On February 16th, Frank's wish finally came through for a two-week furlough. It had been 2 1/2 months since he applied for a furlough and was refused four times. So this was a total surprise when he was told he could leave immediately that day. He found

55

out how cold it was back home, below freezing and a lot of snow. Time sure passed quickly visiting the relatives and again enjoying mom's home cooking.

Figure 50 Frank Home on Furlough

Before he knew it he was on a train and back at Fort Gordon on the 25th after passing through New York City on Tuesday at 7:55 am, Washington at 11:40 am and arriving in Florence, SC at 12:42 am Wednesday. After a long wait in Florence he left at 9:05 pm and arrived at the base close to midnight.

Frank brought his radio back from furlough and wrote on March 3rd, *"I have my radio going strong and have just heard the Chesterfield and also the Camel program. Right now Bob Burns is on. I'm glad I brought the radio back with me as it makes a lot of difference to hear some music, comedy or news once in a while."* Frank got a letter from home telling him the Johnson milk farm hired hand was hit on the road just a few hundred feet from home. The family was listening to the radio in the evening when they heard this horrible scream, which carried well in the cold March air. Three people were walking back from the cow barn when one was hit by a car. Dad and Al rushed out of the house right away and ran to the man that was hit. He was killed instantly, but the other two, a woman and man, were okay. The driver did not stop and to our knowledge never was caught. What a sad, sad circumstance.

During the next few weeks in March, there was a series of events, which were to shape Frank's military career. On March 9th, the First Sergeant notified Frank that he would recommend him for company clerk. Frank wrote home, *"Now I have some good news. Tonight the First Sergeant called me in and asked me how much* schooling I had. I told him, and he wants to recommend me for company clerk. He asked me if I thought I could learn to type. I told him that I believed I could and that I would try my best. He said that was all he asked his men to do. So maybe in the near future, I will be doing some work in the office. I hope so as it might help me after I get out of this army."* As time would tell nothing came of the clerk job, but a few days later the First Sergeant asked if he would like to be an MP, that is Military Police. Frank did not answer yes or no because he was not sure he would like the job. Several other men were asked, and the sergeant said that they would pick the person by looking at the classification files. Frank did not think he could meet the requirements since they required a certain length of service and he only had ten months. He was ordered to report to the Provost Marshall the morning of March 17th to be interviewed as a candidate for the MP position. One other soldier was interviewed as well. Frank was not picked for the MP's but during the next several months he had to serve as an MP guard at the Post Exchange with full uniform and armed. As fate would have it, if Frank had been picked as a full-time MP, he would more than likely not have served on the front lines during the Normandy D-Day invasion.

On March 19th, Frank's buddy Al MacDonald had a very close call while on an overnight problem. Tuesday morning the company had a problem in defense and the men had to dig a foxhole for their protection. Mac picked a place near a barbed wire fence. Suddenly a rainsquall came up, and then a bolt of lightening struck the fence and traveled its entire length. The next thing Mac was conscious of was rain falling on his face and the company commander calling his name. Corporal Gallagher saw Mac fall when the bolt struck, and he ran for the doctor at full speed. By the time the company commander, the doctor and Gallagher got back, Mac was just coming around. Outside of feeling a little weak, Mac was okay.

A few days later on March 23rd, Frank as part of Company C, went on a 20-mile march. He writes, *"I found it wasn't too tough. We had our dinner in the field. Some of the fellows had blisters on their feet before they got back. However I have found that if your shoes are in good shape and you have a pair of clean socks you will be pretty safe from getting blisters while on a march."* When he returned to base, he received good news that he had been promoted to private first class which pays $6 more per month. It also is a stepping-stone to the next higher rating, which is corporal. Frank writes, *"I suppose it will be a long time before I am corporal. The company has quite a few corporals now, and there are only so many allotted to each company."* Well, it was only two days later that Frank was called before the Battalion Commander, Captain Richardson, who informed him that he had a good record, and he would recommend him for corporal. The promotion would include a pay raise of $34 more per month. Two days later, March 28th, the order came through from Colonel Bagby, promoting him to corporal. He now became second in command of the 3rd Squad. When he returned to barracks that night, he found his bed changed around, a typical joke by the men. Amazing that Frank went from private to corporal in just five days. He, indeed, had an excellent record! Then to top it off he got a bonus check from the Jell-O Company for $13.36 for working four months in 1941. At this point life may have been hard in the army, but it was going very well all things considered.

Figure 51 Eleanor Thielman

Then Frank received a letter from an 11-year old girl in Buffalo, NY, enclosing a medal and a prayer. Her name was Eleanor Thielman and was in 5th grade at St. Agnes Catholic School. The sister passed out slips with names of soldiers, and she got Frank W. Brown. During the war, it was common to give school children the address of a soldier to write to as a pen pal, which would help the morale of the soldier. The first letter started a 2 1/2 year period of letter writing and included receiving lovely gifts from Frank, birthday and valentine cards and several pictures. Eleanor, being the thoughtful and sweet girl that she was sent cards and gifts as well.

Figure 52 Billy's Army Uniform

At this time back home, Billy received an army uniform from his Aunt Francis. When Frank heard, he asked that mom send a picture of Billy in his uniform. Later, Billy got a Navy uniform as well but liked his army one more.

The last of March, the government started to ration gasoline at home. If you were a defense plant worker, you were given an exemption since many drove several miles to work in a defense plant. In Frank's hometown of Le Roy, many drove 25 miles to Rochester and even Buffalo, 50 miles away. Dad qualified for the A-1 sticker which was placed on the windshield of the 1936 Chevy and allowed enough gas to drive to work and church on Sunday with little to spare. Then later in 1942 rationing increased to include sugar, meat, lard, oils, cheese, butter, dried fruits, canned milk, coal, fuel oil and, of course, women's nylons. Scrap metal drives were held, and children were encouraged to pick milkweed since the milkweed would be used to make parachutes. Then came the Victory Gardens where you were encouraged to raise vegetables. At home, it was common for mom and dad to plant a garden every year since jobs and money were always tight. In early April, Frank received word that his cousin, Vic Regone, was going overseas, which turned out to be Iceland and later England. Vic was in the Army Signal Corp as a communication's specialist. In high school, he was building radios and would transmit on the local Rochester radio frequencies, which was illegal, but fun nonetheless. Also in April, Congress passed a bill wherein soldiers no longer needed to place postage stamps on their letters, which were 3 cent stamps for regular letters. On April 7th, Frank as a corporal was now second in command in charge of his squad which consisted of 12 men. He then started many details as an MP at the Post Exchange even though he had not been officially selected as an MP under the Provost Marshall. His job was to keep order in the exchange by standing at the exit door.

Figure 53 Girls from Georgia State College

On Sunday, April 13th, Frank and Vic Santangelo took a bus to Augusta and took pictures while walking around town. While Frank was taking a picture of Vic by the city monument, three girls came up and asked if they could take a picture of both of us. Frank writes home, *"Since they were rather good looking, we consented of course and took some pictures of them also. The girls were from the Georgia State College for Women, which is about a 100 miles from Augusta. They belonged to the choir and had come to Augusta to give a recital Sunday night at the Baptist Church. We bought them a dinner and then we went to the recital. All in all, we had a good time."* Now Frank had taken some 8 mm film of the girls, and some years later when Vic and his wife Rose were visiting mom and dad, Billy showed the film with Vic, Frank, and the girls. The interesting part for Rose was when Vic was hugging one of the girls. Well, that evening when Vic and Rose returned to Rochester, you can be sure Vic got an ear full!

Figure 54 Frank's Target With Good Score

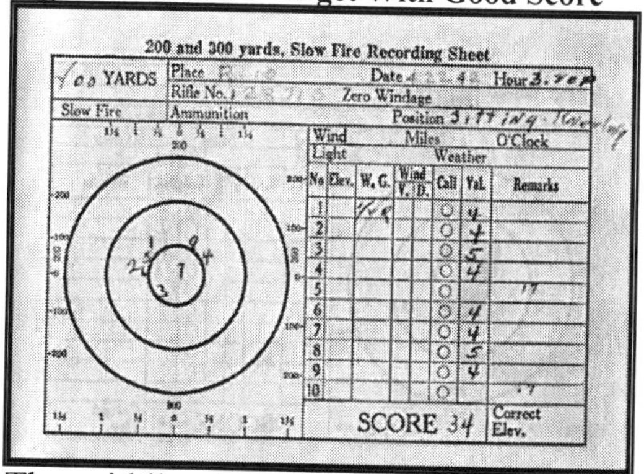

The middle of April started a period of firing the M-1 rifle for record. Frank wrote, "I must get a good score now since I'm a corporal, or I will never hear the end of it." At first, he had a score of 51 out of 60 at 200 yards slow fire. His marksmanship improved and in four days he qualified for marksman by getting 232 points out of 300. He had made a bet with his buddy Mac that the one with low score had to pay the high man a dollar and shine shoes for the winner for one week. Mac lost! Frank came close to qualifying for sharpshooter, but he was a little too anxious.

In Frank's letter home dated April 26th, he enclosed a picture taken in Augusta of Vic Santangelo, Al MacDonald, and Frank. These three men would remain very close from 1942 through D-Day 1944. I met both men after the war on a few occasions, and they were, indeed, men of outstanding character. They both suffered severe injuries from combat in 1944. Vic was struck by rifle fire in the left shoulder while Mac was wounded twice, once being shot through the mouth and later receiving shrapnel in his ankle.

61

Figure 55 Vic, Mac & Frank

Mac remained a private first class while Vic was eventually promoted to First Sergeant of Company C. Later in the war, Vic was awarded the Purple Heart, Bronze Star and Silver Star for bravery in battle.

Figure 56 Mass at Sacred Heart Church

On May 7, 1942, Frank was made squad leader of the 3rd Squad with Corporal Smith second in command and a total of 9 men in the squad. On Mother's Day, May 10th, 500 men of the 4th Division attended services at Sacred Heart Church in Augusta. Afterward, they paraded six blocks to Hotel Richmond where they were served breakfast.

Figure 57 Parade to Hotel Richmond

As reported in the Augusta newspaper, there were two battalions, one commanded by Captain Sasso and the second by Captain Pesnicak. Cadence for the marchers was furnished by the drum and bugle corps of the 12th Infantry under the direction of Sgt. Robert Lloyd. As the marchers neared 8th Street, they passed in review before a reviewing stand upon which Col. Terence Tully, Lt. Col. Herstood, Lt. Col. Thomas Cross, and other officers and members of the clergy including chaplains of the 4th Division. Monsignor Grady, who delivered the principal address told the men that they were not only soldiers of the United States, but also soldiers of Christ and as true soldiers of God and country would bring God back to the world and bring the world back to God.

May would become a month of long marches with 25 miles on May 17th, 18 miles with full pack on May 22, and 20 miles on May 25th. He wrote on the 30th, *"Those hikes (marches) don't bother me much probably because I used to cover a few miles when I went hunting or fishing. We have two barbers down here from N.Y.C., and they have a pretty hard time making those marches. Our Captain also makes the hikes right with us. Once while we were passing near a ditch with some running water in it, he walked*

63

through the water to cool off his feet. We got a kick out of that. He's a real good Captain, though." On the 28th, there was a field problem where artillery was fired overhead into the distant hills. Frank wrote they did not scream like in the movies but sounded like skyrockets.

On June 5, 1942, Frank wrote a letter home clarifying the fact he was writing to a girl in Buffalo. He writes, *"I'm sending you the picture of the girl in Buffalo who sent me the package and who writes to me often. How come you asked if she is good looking? She is just twelve you know! Ha, Ha! Keep this picture for me also as I am going to make a scrapbook with all the pictures I take while I'm in the army."* Then on June 7th, Frank got good news that Dad was doing well and working overtime on his job. The next day the 4th Division marched in a parade for Chief of Staff, General Marshall. There were five columns of vehicles and Frank was car commander of the half-trac and saluted General Marshall as they drove by the reviewing stand. Frank wrote, *"We traveled around 15 mph, and I think our line was pretty even when we went by. We were lucky that our battalion was the first to begin the parade. The other fellows must have eaten a lot of dust. Tonight Mac and I went to Augusta and had a good chicken dinner, southern style. After the dinner, we went to a theater. The picture playing was My Gal Sal. It was pretty fair."*

On June 10th, Frank found out that Dad had sold his LaSalle for $200, and he was very pleased since he had paid $260 for it two years ago. Unfortunately, he was only able to use the car for one year before being drafted. A week later the company commander told Frank he was recommending him for promotion to sergeant. Two days later on June 18th, Frank made sergeant with a pay of $78 per month compared to the corporal pay of $64. He was indeed advancing very fast since he was a private only three months ago. Of course, his responsibilities were increasing as well, but he seemed to be taking this in stride and enjoyed his leadership role. He never complained about the additional responsibility and the problems you come across when you lead other men, especially since these men did not want to be there. In his new role, Frank was now an instructor for weapons training and other duties as well.

On June 20th, the company commander explained the new pay allotments a soldier could make to his family. Frank was in the class B category where the government deducts $22 from his pay and for two parents will add $25, for each sister or brother $5. The payments would not begin until November. Frank wrote, "It seems too good to be true because with my sergeants pay of $78 per month it would be the same as though I was making $113 per month."

On Sunday, June 21st, Frank was MP guard again and had to stop about three fights between men who had a little too much beer. I am unable to document this 100%, but I believe this is when Frank was viciously attacked and came close to being killed by a soldier that had a grudge against him. Frank was returning to barracks when a soldier was hiding behind the barracks door. He struck Frank in the head with an M-1 rifle butt and knocked him unconscious. His barrack mates discovered him, and he was taken to the hospital for treatment. He was struck very close to his temple, and the attack could have been fatal. Vic Santangelo, also a sergeant and Franks friend, found out who the culprit was and when he found the soldier alone he beat the daylights out of him to serve as a lesson to the others. There was a period of two weeks that Frank was recovering and did not write a letter home. Of course, he did not write about the incident at the time because he did not want to worry his parents. A few months later when Frank did get home, mom saw the scar just above and to the side of his eyebrow. When questioned, Frank told the story of what had happened and minimized the injury that he received. However, he knew that he could have been killed. It was indeed a very close call!

Deuteronomy 32:10-11, "He shielded him and cared for him; he guarded him as the apple of his eye like an eagle that stirs up its nest and hovers over its young, that spreads its wings to catch them and carries them on its pinions."

"*****"

Chapter Eight

Carolina Maneuvers
July to August 1942

On July 7, 1942, the Fourth Division started mock battles in South Carolina for three weeks.

Figure 58 Preparing to Move Out

Frank wrote on July 8th, *"Well, here I am on maneuvers again. I left Camp Gordon yesterday morning in a truck convoy. We entered our bivouac area after traveling about 160 miles. It is about eight miles to Pageland SC, the nearest town. The maneuvers won't begin for a few days yet. Meanwhile, we are adjusting ourselves to life in the field. Vic Santangelo and I pitched a tent together. I slept very well last night."* In Figure 59 is one of Frank's best friends, Vic, from Rochester, NY. What a physique!

This cartoon in his July 8th letter shows the sentiment of living in the outdoors on bivouac. The next day Frank writes, *"I got five letters yesterday at our first mail call here. Two letters from you, one from Eleanor, Gertrude Helfrich and John DuBois. You get to appreciate letters more out here than back in the garrison because you are isolated more from everything. It's nearly time for dinner, so I'll have to stop writing and get my mess kit out."*

Figure 59 Vic Santangelo

Figure 60 After Chow Cleanup

In a week, the men were experiencing the rigor of field training. On July 14, 1942, they would break camp at 4:30 am, marched all day and then about 4:00 pm engaged the opposing forces, which they battled until after dark. Frank was so dehydrated that he stopped at a nearby store and purchased four cans of tomato juice, three orange, and one apple juice and drank them all. They ate supper about 11:00 pm and at 2:30 am they were eating breakfast. By 3:30 am they were on the road again and marched until about 8:30 am and made camp. How about that for a day in the infantry!

Well, by the next day Frank was ready for a bath and found a creek nearby for a quick wash. No sooner than he got wet when they got the order to move out fast. He packed so quickly that he thought he lost his glasses.

Figure 61 The 12th Regiment on the Move

He was then attached to the 29th Division and got two days deserved rest near Dilworth, NC. Then on Sunday, July 19th Frank and his buddy Mac decided to approach a farmhouse near their bivouac area and asked the farmer's wife if they could take a bath and wash out some socks. She indeed agreed to their request and afterward insisted they both stay for supper. They paid the nice woman for the excellent dinner even though she did not want any compensation. What an exceptional act of kindness from a stranger. It shows the high degree of respect our citizens showed the armed forces in WWII.

On Monday, July 20th, they moved by truck convoy to a bivouac area between Pageland, SC, and Monroe, NC. They would stay in this area for a few days occupied with lectures and field practice. After pitching their tents Frank, Vic and Sgt. Works went looking for a creek to take a bath. They found a pond about a mile away, and it was deep enough to swim, so they had a good swim beside the bath. That night they had quite a bit of ice cream at camp and boy did that taste good. In the evening, the USO showed a Hollywood movie with a 16 mm projector in an open field. It was a good movie. That day Frank found his lost glasses. They were in his gas mask carrier, and he had been carrying them all the time he thought they were lost.

Figure 62 Frank Enjoying Moment of Rest

On July 21st, the company commander bought fifty watermelons for the company, and each man got a fourth of a watermelon for breakfast. He also purchased some beer, which they had with their noon meal. Don't think for a moment that this was standard army issue. The company had a fund that was used to buy extra food for the men. It sure helped the morale of the men. Frank writes, *"These maneuvers aren't as hard as being in garrison and they certainly aren't harder than the last maneuvers. I am quite accustomed to living in the field. It isn't as bad as it sounds. The only thing that the men find hard is that they don't get many chances to get to a town or a city."*

July 24th was a day to practice making quick fortifications, which involved digging foxholes and slit trenches. That is quite a foxhole that Frank dug.

Figure 63 Frank's Perfect Foxhole

Can you imagine digging down through tree roots, stones, and hard clay, only to move on the next day, set up camp and do it all over? No wonder the infantry was considered to make a man out of a boy. Then an iceman came around, in the middle of nowhere, selling ice cream, tomato juice, etc. The men now experienced many salesmen coming to the bivouac area selling candy, ice cream, cakes, watermelons, and newspapers. There was no problem selling their wares to hungry GI's tired of rations and field army food.

Figure 64 Frank With Maps

That night Frank and Vic got a ride on a convoy going into Charlotte, which was 26 miles from camp. The only problem was it left at 8:30 pm and when they reached the city it was 10:00 pm. They had to be back to the trucks at 12:00 am, so there was only enough time to go to a restaurant and have a good dinner. Vic got that wonderful southern fried chicken and Frank had delicious lamb chops, and that's when lamb chops were cheaper than steak. The next day Frank and Vic went to a nearby farm and borrowed two wash tubs and did their laundry. They were glad to get that finished, as there were quite a bundle of dirty clothes. When the laundry was done, they both bought a watermelon from a local black boy and devoured it. Frank bought some kerosene, a wick and made light with a tomato can. He wrote, *"It's more of a smudge pot than a lamp, but it throws enough light to write by. I have the lamp just outside of the tent, so that I won't be smoked out."*

Figure 65 Hide and Seek in the Woods

One day the platoon had to do post duty, where they were strung out in a long line in groups of threes and fours to guard against an attack. They were not likely to have supper that night since the kitchen truck was lost somewhere in the area. Frank wrote, *" Well I was getting just a little hungry when Kollar comes up to me and gives me a tomato and a cucumber he had swiped from a farmer's field nearby. That tomato sure tasted good."* On Sunday, the 26th, Frank and Vic went to a slate quarry about two miles from camp and took a bath even though the water was a little dirty. Afterward they attended a field Sunday service, which was interrupted by some sun and rain. On Tuesday the 31st, Frank writes, *"We arrived at Camp Gordon about three this afternoon. Until now I have been busy getting my bed set up and my equipment and clothes in order. We made the trip back in good time without many stops as we have experienced before. Tomorrow is payday. I imagine half of the 4th Division will be in town tomorrow night. I'm going to a movie here in camp instead."*

The following is taken from a newspaper account of the maneuvers titled, Troops Face 2nd Week of Mock War, With the

First Army in the Carolinas (AP). *"Weary and field worn from five days of mock warfare, the soldiers of Lieut. Gen. Hugh A. Drums's Blue First Army began today a weekend of rest in preparation for another week of battle, the windup of the year's maneuver schedule. Simulated warfare in the 10,000 square mile maneuver area in the Carolinas will be resumed Monday or Tuesday. In the meantime, the 200,000 men of the Blue Army and the 100,000 of Maj. Gen. Oscar W. Griswold's Red Fourth Corps will refurbish their equipment and move to new concentration areas. Neither commander has been advised of the final problem to be handed him by Army General Headquarters. The first phase of the GHQ maneuvers ended yesterday with the Blue forces encircling the fast moving mechanized columns of General Griswold on the North, the East, and the South. For five full days, the soldiers of the opposing sides had struggled with little rest and often with little food except emergency rations. General Drum said that the First Army's newly developed tank-attacker units were largely responsible for his success over the Red first and second armored divisions, stymied in every effort to flank or break through First Army defenses. These attacks consisted of 75 and 35 mm guns mounted on fast moving trucks, engineer, infantry, and aviation forces. Although praising them, General Drum declined to say that they were the answer to the question of how tanks should be dealt with. Some improvements in the present makeup were indicated, he said. General Griswold, with an Army of only half the Blue strength, had under his command the nation's only two complete armored divisions, its only completely motorized infantry division and superiority in medium bombers."*

Following that article was another by General Griswold titled, General Griswold Lauds Fourth Corps, With the Fourth Corps in the Carolinas (AP). *"The highest praise for the 100,000 men who carried out orders with spirit and enthusiasm came today from Maj. Gen. Oscar W. Griswold, commander of the Fourth Corps, which met the First Army in a week's training battle just over. "I believe we are on the way to getting ready,"* the general said. *"The basic thing is that the Army is on sound lines and when bullets begin to fly many other things will straighten out automatically."* In summary, the highlight of the Carolina maneuvers for the 4th Division was a well executed several hundred-mile trip. On this motor trip were some 2,300 vehicles carrying a complement of 15,000 men." The Carolina Maneuvers were now completed.

Philippians 4:19, "And my God will meet all your needs according to his glorious riches in Christ Jesus."

"****"

Chapter Nine

Return to Camp Gordon
August 1942 to April 1943

On August 3, 1942, Frank received a letter from home that Al, his brother, would be inducted into the army soon. The dread of many parents throughout the nation was to have more than one son serve in harms way. It was not uncommon to have two or three serving at one time and in a few instances as many as five, such as the Sullivan brothers that were all lost on the same Navy ship.

Frank wrote on August 3rd, *"Mac and I went to Augusta and after church we had a chicken dinner, then a show and after the show, we had another chicken dinner. Vic, Mac and I had talked about southern fried chicken so much while we were on maneuvers that we had worked up quite an appetite for chicken. It was pretty warm in Augusta yesterday. The temperature was over 95 degrees. We drilled for an hour this morning and the remainder of the day we spent cleaning the barracks. So you see besides being able to help you with the washing I can help scrub the floors. We have to keep these barracks pretty clean because if the Major finds even a little dust on the shelves, there's the devil to pay."* Oh boy, that sure brings back memories when I was in USAF basic training. We scrubbed the floors, windows, and everywhere dust could settle, and we got dinged in an inspection when our superior officer found dust in a knothole. Would you believe that?

On August 5th, Frank wrote his brother Al and gave him some advice on the army. *"Now for a little advice. You will find that the first six or eight weeks in the army are your hardest. They will give you plenty of work to do. Sometimes you may think you are getting more than your share of it, but just keep quiet and do it. You will run into some no good corporals and sergeants. Don't let them get under your skin. Do whatever they tell you. Sooner or later you will be shifted into a different squad and will have a different noncom over you. Most of the noncoms are okay, but you are bound* to run into a bad one. When you leave, it will be a good idea to take three or four suits of underwear. The Army will issue you four suits, but a few extra suits of underwear will come in handy. Take along ten or twenty dollars. You will find that there are some extra things you need, and you also will have some money if you want to go to a show. Remember the sizes of your clothing so when they issue you your uniform and clothes, you won't have to guess the size. Don't forget to write me and home too and let me know how you are getting along." Frank's advice sounds good for any soldier entering the military.

Now back at Camp Gordon, the marches started again. Frank was proud of his ability to march for 19 or even 24 miles and ration his water to one canteen only. On August 8th, he wrote, *"Friday we marched 20 miles. It was the easiest hike we made yet. Our company made it 100 percent. If the battalion had made it 100 percent, we would have had a day off, but one man from Co. B couldn't come in under his own power, so we didn't get the day off. All the officers went all the way on their shoe leather this time too. That's something unusual. I went all the way without touching my canteen. We were only supposed to have one canteen of water for the March. The canteen when full holds one quart of water. If a soldier can learn how to save his water and how to drink it, he need not fear a long march. After we got back and had supper, I went to the post exchange and bought a quart of ice cream. It sure hit the spot."*

On August 11th, Frank received a package of cookies from back home, which occurred quite often with mom, aunts and friends sending tasty goodies. He also received a package from the Jell-O Recreational Club. They sent six packs of cigarettes, comb, handkerchief and candy. Frank had no use for the cigarettes but I'm sure traded them for more candy. On Sunday afternoon, Vic and Frank went to Augusta and Vic took Frank to see Mr. And Mrs. Door. They were a very nice couple with a baby and a small girl. They took Frank and Vic to the Elks Club and treated them to a barbecue chicken dinner. Above is a picture of Frank taken in front of Doors home. There were several invitations to the Doors over the weeks ahead. Frank wrote on August 23d, *"We had a nice fish fry at the Doors last night. Mr. Door had some fish his neighbor had caught and he cooked them outside over a charcoal fire. We also ate some (redhorse). Redhorse is a mixture of corn meal, buttermilk, onions, and catsup. It is fried in fat like fish, and it tastes real good."* Frank and Vic were getting a good exposure to southern cooking.

Figure 66 Frank at Door's Home

Figure 67 Door's Lovely Daughter

Frank received a letter from home on August 15th, saying that Al was rejected for health reasons when he was given his physical. Al was disappointed, but his parents were happy since they did not want another son in the army at this time. The next day Vic, Mac, and Frank went to Augusta, saw the movie "Ships Ahoy" with Eleanor Powell and had a southern fried chicken dinner afterward. The next day they had a full field inspection where they all marched out to the parade ground and pitched tents. Officers inspected the equipment for serviceability. No word on how the inspection came out.

Frank experienced disappointment with one of his men in his squad in mid-August. He went over the hill; that is AWOL for ten days. He said he just got tired of waiting for a furlough, so he took one on his own. Unfortunately, it doesn't work that way in the army or any military service. Frank writes, *"The bad part is that he will*

Figure 68 Mr. & Mrs. Door

Figure 69 Field Inspections

have to stand trial. I hope they go easy on him because he is the best soldier I have in my squad and a nice fellow." A week later, Frank took the soldier who went AWOL to the battalion commander. The Major sentenced him to 30 days hard labor and fined him $18. Men sentenced to hard labor have to work from 7:00 to 10:00 pm every night so they never have any free time for themselves. The work usually consists of scrubbing building floors or doing other cleaning jobs. Frank wrote, *"It is a real punishment but its better than having to go to the stockade."*

When in the field on practice problems, Frank was always on the lookout for arrowheads in a farmer's plowed field. He was successful on two occasions when he found white arrowheads. He wrote on September 6th, *"While I was out in the woods I found another arrowhead. This is a pure white one and will look nice in my collection."*

Figure 70 Frank's Arrowhead Collection

Now at home something happened that caught Frank's attention. As part of the war effort civilians were encouraged to set up air observation posts to observe the skies for enemy aircraft. The observation posts were mainly a propaganda effort to engage the civilian population to be more conscious and involved in the war effort. Back home in Le Roy, one farmer got so enthused that he took aim at an aircraft overhead and shot it full of holes. When the news reached Frank from home, he wrote back, *"I told some of the fellows here about the farmer who shot up that airplane. They got quite a laugh of that. They are all of the opinions that if he is caught, he should be sent into the armed forces. They can always use men who can shoot at airplanes and hit them too."*

On September 17, 1942, Frank was notified by the First Sergeant that he would have to be color guard for the battalion parade later in the day. He reported to the Major for instruction and had only one hour to change his uniform and study the color sergeant's duties, get the colors and report to the company commander. Frank carried the colors and had a private on both sides with rifles. He wrote later that he got through the ceremonies okay but was darn glad when the parade was over. The author recalls facing the same situation when in USAF summer camp at Ethan Allen Air Force Base at Winooski, VT. I was asked to prepare for the same duty the night before a parade and was given the manual on the exact procedure, commands and correct response all in proper sequence. The night watch woke me up at 4:00 am and I studied the book to every detail. The procedure was four pages long, and all of this had to be memorized in proper sequence. The next day it was bright and sunny, and when the time came, I was scared I would make a mistake. At the appropriate time, I started the command sequence to the receiving officer and then my mind went blank. What else could I do but try to fake it. The receiving officer's face went white and very much confused maybe since he did not know the proper sequence as well. When finished we were asked to report to the company commander who reprimanded us for such a poor performance. So the author appreciates what his brother went through, for his brother was a far better man than he was.

In early September the 12th Regiment got a new commander, Lt Colonel Homs. Frank wrote, *"He seems like the best one we have had yet. He says that he wants the men to have furloughs and that he thinks that we should have a better recreation hall, more entertainment, and parties. So I may get a furlough before Christmas yet."* Now, who wouldn't like a commander like that? By mid-September 1942, Frank learned that he was in line soon for a furlough home. In a letter dated September 20, 1942, he asked his parents for a little money so he could pay for his train fare home and needed to have his suitcase shipped in time for his furlough. Then on September 22nd, he wrote that he was learning to drive a half-trac. There were 43,000 of these vehicles built in America in WWII and were very versatile in the field. He said, *"These machines are like a big truck. They are plenty heavy. I enjoyed driving it. I had to learn the shift, which is a little different than the car shift, and also have to double clutch while shifting. The Lieutenant gave me a test and said that I did okay. We also learned some Judo this morning. It's a form of wrestling."*

The next day Frank got his furlough home for two weeks from September 24 to October 4th. It was a wonderful time of the year to be home. Dad was just finishing up the grape harvest and was in the process of making 200 gallons of red wine. Fresh tomatoes were still available along with those early fall apples. Frank spent his time with the family and many of his relatives and friends in the Le Roy, NY area. He always wanted to see his pen pal, Eleanor Thielman in Buffalo, but time went so fast he was never able to meet her and her family in person. While Frank was home, he got a letter from Vic at Camp Gordon telling him when he left it turned very cold and they had much rain. Vic then informs Frank that they had another incident on Friday night with old Davis. He apparently tried the same thing on Mills as he tried on Taylor. Vic does not say

Figure 71 Frank on Fall Furlough

what this infraction was except that it was bad enough that he did everything but throw him out of the barracks. Mills didn't even want to touch him not wanting to hurt the old guy. Evidently Davis must have done some pretty bad things since the men won't even look at him anymore. Frank never wrote home about such things, since he did not want to worry his parents that you sometimes have to live with some terrible people. Vic also mentions that the new regimental commander, Lieutenant Colonel Homs, told the men that he was very proud of them and the good work they have been doing. He said that when he took charge there were only 53 men on furlough, and now there are 457. Also, there were 53 men in the guardhouse, and now there are only 10. This man sure knew how to improve the proficiency and morale of the regiment. When Frank returned, he got right back into the training. However that night, October 5th, he wrote, *"The boys were just chasing a mouse around the barracks. They finally caught it. More darn excitement over a little mouse. Tell Billy he should have his little cat here."*

In the fall of 1942, after Frank returned from his furlough, morning physical training was changed to a one-mile run every morning before breakfast with rifle and packs. They started with a few hundred yards but soon were lengthened to one mile. Another routine was the barrack inspection one or two times per week. Preparation for barrack inspection included scrubbing the floors with brushes until they were white, placing all personal gear in exact order including the clothes on the racks and, of course, having your rifle cleaned with not a speck of dirt shown. If the company captain found a speck of dirt or dust anywhere, they would have to clean again. One time the inspector was General McNair, and that is considered high-level. Training consisted of weekly field problems, which usually lasted two or three days and then one or two parades a week. The parades usually occurred on Saturday or Sunday afternoon, with the public invited from Augusta and after a while they became boring.

Weekly assigned duties could be Orderly Room CQ or MP at the Post Exchange. In November 1942, Frank was selected along with another sergeant from the company to attend weapons school for eight days. There was a test upon completion, and he then would be qualified to instruct the rest of Company C. Frank studied very carefully putting in two additional hours per day practicing on various weapons. Besides the written test Frank had to field strip five weapons "blindfolded" and then assemble them. He passed the test with a "Very Satisfactory" grade and was now a qualified instructor.

Usually, on weekends, the men would have plenty of time to socialize, and play sports like baseball, volleyball, football or basketball. Sometimes it was just plain fun to horse around which the following pictures, taken by Frank, clearly show.

Figure 72 Ready ...Catch

81

Figure 73 Mock Drill

Figure 74 Under the Bridge

Figure 75 Cigarette and Latest Rumor

Figure 76 Surrender?

Many times the men would just gather to have a cigarette and catch up on the latest rumor or scoop of the day. Rumors were freely given, sounded good nevertheless and took away from the daily routine. The weekends were used up with parades especially when there was a visiting high-ranking officer such as a general. This picture shows a visiting general giving a speech to the Fourth Division on November 11, 1942, with about 14,000 in attendance. Hope it was a good talk to rally the troops and not a complete bore.

Figure 77 General Giving Speech

The city of Augusta was a perfect place to be close to when stationed at Camp Gordon. There were many good restaurants, the YMCA, USO Club, several movie theaters and the very hospitable Door family who made good friends with Frank, Vic, and Mac. Frank took many movies and still pictures in Augusta of his friends and landmarks.

Figure 78 Time for Watermelon

Figure 79 Swim at Augusta Park

Figure 80 Frank in Augusta Park

The weekend routine usually included a visit to Augusta for a good chicken or steak dinner. Augusta restaurants were usually very crowded, especially after paydays, and you would have to stand at the door patiently waiting for a table. Frank and his friends usually saw two to three movies per week, many of which were war films, most very poorly made and regarded primarily as propaganda films. However movies were a great escape from the reality of war for the soldiers as well as the general public, and the admission in town was cheap around 35 to 50 cents a ticket. Frank would often comment in his letters on the movies he saw and provided his personal rating.

Figure 81 Frank in Downtown Augusta

On November 8th, Frank received a new Kodak camera from his brother Al who now had a job at Kodak in Rochester. With the new camera, he started taking pictures right away of Camp Gordon, his buddies and on visits to Augusta.

Figure 82 Frank With Girls in Augusta

The highlight of November was the Thanksgiving Dinner on the 26th. They had all the turkey they wanted, stuffed olives, potatoes, cranberry sauce, gravy, stuffing, celery stalks stuffed with pimento cheese, fruit cake, pie, nuts, candy, fruit and ice cream. Frank wrote, *"I ate almost enough to last until Christmas."*

The month of December 1942 started out real busy for Frank. After being qualified as a weapons trainer, he was now giving instruction on the Browning automatic rifle. Then General Lear arrived, inspected Company C and then reviewed the 4th Division in the afternoon parade. Afterward, General Barton informed the soldiers that General Lear was well pleased with the division and everyone could have the entire day off tomorrow. Besides that, they don't have to get up for reveille and breakfast would be at 8:00 am. Wow, that is something in the army! However all the noncoms, which included Frank, had to assemble at the sports arena at 9:00 am to hear General Lear speak.

Figure 83 4th Division on Parade

In November, Frank's brother-in-law, Mannie Costa was inducted in the Army Air Corp and after a few weeks at the Niagara Falls Induction Center, he was sent to a base near Atlantic City. His wife Eleanor and her sister Mary took a train trip to the army base to see him for a few days before he was sent to a base in South Dakota for radio training. Later Mannie wrote Frank that the weather in South Dakota was frigid with temperatures 10 to 15 degrees below zero.

On December 6th, Frank wrote a letter to his sister Mary advising her not to go muskrat trapping like he used to do when he was home. Apparently she was thinking of doing some trapping to earn a few extra dollars in selling the pelts. Frank wrote, *"To be sure you might possibly earn a few dollars but there are a few things that you may not have considered. You may get a nasty cold if you get wet setting traps. I can still remember chopping a hole in the ice and then searching for a trap with my arm in the water almost to my* shoulder. When I did that a few times, my arm would turn quite blue. Once too, I broke through the ice and got a boot full of ice water. Bought a toy for Billy at Sears and had it mailed from the store. While I'm on this subject, I would like you to send me your sizes, mothers and Eleanor's." A few days later Frank got a Christmas package from the Jell-O Company with a stamp on it saying, "Do not open until Christmas." Frank wrote, *"After I get back from our night problem and if I'm hungry, I think I may unwrap it."* On December 11th, Frank received some good news that he made the highest mark in the regiment on the weapons test. No doubt his hard study paid off. He then opened the package from Jell-O and to his delight, he found quite a few useful gifts. There was a good toothbrush, large size tube of toothpaste, a jar of shaving cream, identification tag chain, handkerchief, a pack of playing cards, a pair of dice, ten packs of cigarettes, candy and soap. Frank writes, *"The cards are already in service as I write for some of the boys are using them in a little blackjack game. I gave the cigarettes to Vic and George."* Frank did not smoke!

Frank was hoping for a furlough to go home for Christmas but knew the chances were slim, since, in 1941, he had to wait until February. Then on December 14th, George Stencovage, acting First Sergeant, told Frank that they were not getting furloughs until after the holidays. Just as Frank was not expecting a furlough, to his surprise the next day he got a two-week furlough to spend time with the family at Christmas. It was sure great being home for Christmas, the first in two years. Billy got a Marx electric train set from Santa, which, of course, was on his Santa list. Mom made Frank's favorite home-style meals, and there were many visits to relatives and friends. Time went way too fast. Frank returned to camp on December 29, 1942, with Bob Leonard by traveling all night and arriving at 5:00 am. The next day an order came through that all furloughs were canceled. Frank was very fortunate to get one when he did.

Figure 84 Billy, Mom, Frank & Dad Christmas 1942

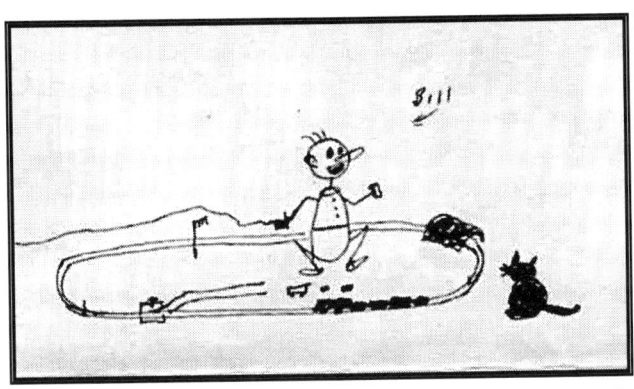

Frank got right back into the routine by going to the range to fire the rifle and machine gun, a few winks in the afternoon and then went on MP duty at the Post Exchange. While he was home, at camp he had received his Christmas packages from mom, sister Eleanor, Eleanor Thielman, and about fifty Christmas cards. At this time, Frank was assigned to a different barracks where he would share a room with Sgt. Stencovage. It was better than the squad room as he now can keep the light on after ten to write letters.

Frank started 1943 with receiving an unexpected bonus check from the Jell-O Company for $24.75. He did not work a single hour in 1942 at the Jell-O Company and got the bonus check regardless, so he was very thankful for their generosity and the high respect Jell-O had for their soldiers. He also got a copy of the New Testament designed with a lesson or chapter for each day of the year. The year started out with Frank continuing to provide instruction on the rifle range, and a new submachine gun. In early January 1943, the regiment started a buddy system when on a pass, where they are grouped together in threes and when one man signs out his two buddies must go as well. If one applies for a pass, all three of them get the pass. The purpose of this system was to ensure that at least one fellow will stay sober enough to keep the other two out of trouble and see that they also get back to camp in time. The buddies must stay together no matter where they go. There was plenty of joking about this rule, and you can bet Frank, Vic and Mac signed as buddies.

On January 12, 1943, the day started out with a field problem and in the afternoon, they ran a new obstacle course, about two miles long. Most of it was in the swamp, and they had to cross a creek about six times by walking over logs or by ropes. About half of the men fell in the creek including Frank. Their clothes were covered with mud, and some tore their clothes from the barbed wire. One of the obstacles was a series of tunnels they had to go through. The fellow in front of Frank leading him took a wrong turn, and they were in the tunnel for about a half hour. They apparently were traveling in a big circle and finally figured out how to escape the maze. As a result, their rifles were quite dirty from sand and mud. It took Frank three hours to clean his M-1 Garand rifle that night.

Mom wrote on January 10th, that Billy climbed a large cherry tree in the back yard. He climbed as high as he could, and when he looked down became scared and was afraid of falling. So here it was below zero outside, and all Billy could do was scream, *"Mommy, Mommy, help me."* After some time, she went out to look for him and had to climb the cherry tree to bring him down. Now that must have been a sight since mom had not climbed a cherry tree in many years. Frank loved to draw cartoons of his brother Billy, so here is one of him in that cherry tree.

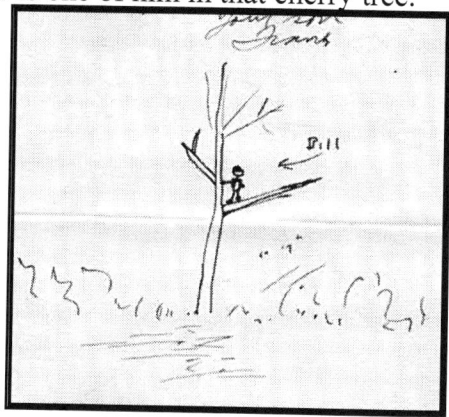

He also drew one of Billy throwing a football to his sister Mary and hitting her in the head. That must have hurt a little. Then there was

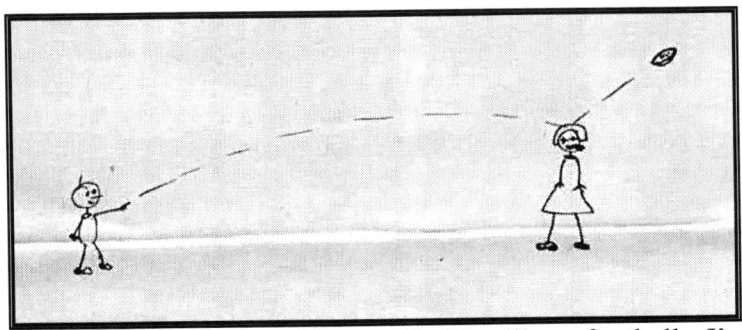

the attempt by Billy to use his cat Blackie, like a football. I'm sure Blackie did not even get close for that drill.

Every week in January was spent on at least three-night problems providing instruction on weapons like the 50 caliber machine gun. On February 1st, Frank had an incident in the barracks where he had to take immediate action to stop a soldier from breaking up the place. The soldier was drunk and threw a shoe through the window in the downstairs door. Frank had to subdue him, involving quite a struggle, and call the MP's to place him in the stockade. Frank wrote, *"Some fellows go completely wild when they get full of whiskey."* No statement could be truer than that. Makes one wonder how such a person would behave in the front battle lines. At about this time the company was starting to cancel furloughs. Mac and Bob Leonard had their bags packed and ready to go when they got the word they were not going. This was indeed quite a disappointment.

Now Frank continued to receive goodie packages from home and when they arrived, in his kind nature, would share them with whoever was present. Some soldiers never received mail or packages with candy or cookies, and I'm sure Frank felt sorry for them. The candy Frank received was usually from one of two candy stores in Le Roy called Tountas and Ellis candies. Both men were Greek, and I remember how good their candies were. Sgt. DeLabovi could not get over the quality of the candy and liked it so much he would offer Frank money for it. Frank could have had a side business going if he wanted to. At the beginning of February 1943, the company continued their day or night practice problems. Frank wrote on February 7th, *"Friday we left camp and were on a two-day field problem. We didn't get back till about seven last night. It rained all night Friday, and my rifle was pretty badly rusted, so all this morning I spent cleaning my rifle. This afternoon I slept for three and a half hours. I had intended to write some letters, but I was just too sleepy. Between yesterday and today's mail call, I received eight letters. Much of my free time this week will be taken up answering them. However it's nice that I get letters!"*

On February 10, 1943, Vic and Frank went to Augusta to eat their usual chicken dinner. However, they had a difficult time finding a drug store that had any ice cream. After the third try, they were able to get a couple of sundaes. It seems that ice cream is being rationed. The irony of it was that all the liquor stores they passed were well stocked. Frank heard that back home gasoline was being rationed, and pleasure driving was now forbidden. Shame they couldn't use alcohol in their gas tanks. Frank continued his practice of wiring extra money home telling his parents to use any of it that they needed and to place the rest of it in his bank account.

Frank and Vic had put in for a three-day pass, and it came through unexpectedly Friday night, February 12th. They wanted to take a trip to Atlanta and see the sights. A three-day pass was limited to 150 miles from camp and Atlanta was within that limit. The next day their trip got off to a bad start when Vic picked up his suitcase from the railway express agent in Atlanta. Upon opening the suitcase, he found that his wristwatch was missing. The thief knew right where to cut the bag to steal the watch. Vic would file a claim, but it would take some time before he would be reimbursed. Unfortunately, this type of theft was very common since many soldiers were traveling home or station to station.

Their first day in Atlanta turned out to be quite cold and windy. After going to church in the morning, they went to the USO Club, which in their view was the best they have seen in the South. They stayed at the YMCA and on Sunday afternoon they visited the museum where there was a gigantic painting showing the Battle of Atlanta during the Civil War. The painting is 50 ft in height and about 300 ft long. It is suspended on a circular wall, and the spectators view it from a circular platform. In the foreground are figures of wax life-sized soldiers, horses, cannon, trees, and shrubs. Frank wrote, *"When looking at the picture you can't tell where the picture ends and the foreground begins, it is so well blended. From one spot on the platform, you are supposed to see 30 miles of landscape. A lecturer gives a short talk describing the picture and it really was worth seeing."*

The author saw the same painting in 1963 when on a NASA business trip to Atlanta. The painting was everything that Frank describes. An interesting trivia about this painting was that there was a small wax figure of Clark Gable, who played Rhett Butler in the movie Gone With The Wind. The film was adapted from the famous book by the same title, written by Margaret Mitchell, a resident of Atlanta, GA.

When Frank and Vic arrived back to camp on Monday, Frank found four letters waiting for him and three boxes of candy: one from mom, Aunt Fran and another from Aunt Lucy Longhany. Frank sent and received quite a few Valentines over Valentine's Day. He always enjoyed sending out birthday and holiday cards. The Valentine below, he sent to his pen pal in Buffalo, Eleanor Thielman.

The next valentine was sent to his brother Billy.

In late February 1943 first war tragedy to strike the extended family occurred. Frank's Aunt Lucy had a son in the Navy just a few years younger than Frank. Aunt Lucy was mom's sister that lived in Lime Rock, NY, just a few miles East of Le Roy. Lucy and Peter Longhany had three boys and three girls.

Figure 85 Richard Longhany

Richard the oldest was 21 and enlisted August 22, 1942, in the Navy. He became Seaman First Class and trained at the Great Lakes Naval Training Station, Armory Gunnery School in Chicago, IL. In February 1943, he was serving as a gunner on a merchant ship in a convoy in the North Atlantic. Convoys of merchant ships were supplying England and other Allies such as Russia with vital war materials produced in the USA. Germany at this time had developed an extensive submarine fleet to sink these ships wherever they were sighted. On February 23, 1943, Richard's ship was torpedoed without warning at night. The crew abandoned ship in lifeboats and rafts, and the Germans took some prisoners on board their submarine. Richard apparently never made it to the lifeboats and his family was told later that his death was certain. Eddy Longhany, Richard's brother, informed the author that he talked to one of the survivors that lived in Connecticut. The survivor told Eddy that he hid in the darkness from the Germans since he did not want to be taken as a prisoner of war. He survived on a raft in the frigid North Atlantic for a few days and was very fortunate to be picked up by another convoy. Now that decision took an incredible amount of courage!

Richard's family was not notified until two months later, April 22, 1943, that he was *"missing in action, somewhere at sea."* A year later, February 1944, they were notified that his ship had been torpedoed February 23, 1943. Little did Frank's parents realize that in a little over a year, in mid-1944, they would face the same tragedy of not knowing the fate of their son Frank. Richard N. Longhany was awarded the American and European Campaign Medals, Purple Heart and others for giving his life for his country.

In early March, one of the soldiers in the company came down with measles. A quarantine was ordered on the whole company, that is, restrictions on passes for visits to Augusta. They were inspected every day for two weeks until the measles were no longer detected. Then on Sunday, March 7, 1943, Company C was notified that they would be going on a two-week maneuver next week. Frank looked forward to the out-of-camp training and called it a little vacation. He went to the service club's cafeteria and enjoyed a good steak dinner for $.55, which he thought was a good price. A steak in Augusta is never less than $1.25. I remember as well while serving in the USAF getting great dinners at the officer's club and for a very low price. That is where I took my date, followed by a dance afterward with a live band at no additional cost.

Figure 86 Bivouac Maneuvers

On March 8, 1943, they started the two-week maneuvers. Frank took his camera to get some good shots of the training event. Frank wrote, *"Hmm it seems as though Dad made some good wine this year. Or do you and Eleanor just sip a little to keep warm those cold nights? Ha, Ha! Well, probably tomorrow night I'll wish I had some wine to keep me warm. But, if there is enough of wood around, I will make sure to have a nice little fire in front of my tent. I have a carton of twenty packs of gum in my field pack. I understand that it's hard to buy outside of camp. If you can't get any home, let me know for I can buy all I want at the PX."* Frank's next letter came from a bivouac, 12 miles from Abbeville, SC. He wrote, *"We are bivouacked in a nice area, and I have a mattress of pine needles in my tent that is almost as good as goose feathers. I have my three blankets and my overcoat, so I keep nice and warm at night. We leave our bivouac area every day and go out on different problems. This forest we are camped in is the Sumpter National Forest."*

Figure 87 Maneuvers Somewhere in South Carolina

March 12th, Friday AM - *"Having a good deal of rain. 10-mile march canceled. The movie last night in the field, Parachute Battalion, not very good."*

March 13th, Saturday PM - *"Company had a beer party. There were 50 cases of beer on hand, and they finished it all much to my surprise. Many of the men didn't wait for the beer party but went to Greenwood and Abbeville instead. So those that remained had too much beer."*

March 14th, Sunday PM - *"Sgt. Delabovi and I came to Greenwood this afternoon. It is about 30 miles from our bivouac area. This town is about the size of Le Roy, but it is pretty well crowded with servicemen today. They have an army band giving a concert near the Railway station. Sgt. Delabovi and I visited the American Legion hall here to take a shower."*

March 17th, Wednesday PM - *"Considerable rain. This morning we had a lesson on tanks. We had to crouch in a foxhole* and let a tank go over the top of it. It really was very safe because that sort of thing has been done before and the holes are always measured to see if they are deep enough for safety."

March 18th, Thursday PM - *"It rained again today, so we didn't do much. We are having supper an hour earlier tonight so that the men can attend a dance in Greenwood. I was going to go down tonight to get a warm shower at the high school in that town, but I am still undecided."*

March 21st, Monday PM - *"Your box of cookies arrived OK Saturday night, just at the right time too because I was as hungry as a wolf after our trip back to camp. We left our camp at Sumpter National Forrest about 10:00 AM Saturday and reached Camp Gordon about 3:00 PM."*

Back at Camp Gordon, Frank started a 10-day reading course on foreign maps and wrote, *"We study maps made by foreign countries. Some of them differ greatly from the map system of ours. It is something different that I find interesting."* On March 27th, Vic, Mac, and Frank went to Augusta Saturday night and visited the Door family. Paul Door made some catfish chowder and roasted some peanuts, popped corn and made some chocolate cookies. Frank wrote, *"We had an enjoyable evening. Then when we were about to leave they insisted we remain there overnight. Finally, we did and this morning we went to services in Augusta."* What a testimony for a fantastic young couple to share their home with a few of the military. I'm sure by now the Doors are deceased, but it sure would be great to pass on our thanks to the family members. The visit was the last time that Frank and his buddies would see the Doors since a change of station was coming up soon.

March 31st, Frank wrote his brother Al telling him that he was again cleaning his M-1 Garand rifle. He wrote, *"You really have to take good care of a rifle especially after firing it. The rifle bore has to be cleaned three times after firing to prevent it from pitting. I've had my M-1 ever since I was in Ft Benning a year and a half ago, and it is in perfect condition. I am glad to hear that you have met a nice girl. If I ain't an old fossil by the time I get out of this army, I'll have to find myself one."* In a very short time, Frank would be in contact with a wonderful girl.

In early April 1943, Frank wrote home with the surprise that they would soon have a permanent change of station to Ft Dix in New Jersey. It was good news since he would be much closer to home and could probably get home on a three-day pass. Of course, the New York City men were overjoyed since Ft Dix is very close to the city. On April 6th, Frank gave a lecture to the company on reconnaissance patrols, which usually the officers would teach, but all the officers had other duties that day. On April 8th, Frank wrote not to worry about him taking a foreign map reading course because this is standard training in the army. With news daily on the war, mom was now facing the fact that her son would eventually be placed in the war zone.

Now back home Billy received a puppy from Uncle Bill, and Frank wrote mom to send a picture of Billy with his new pal. Well, that is precisely what Billy named his first dog, "Pal".

Figure 88 Billy and Dog Pal

On April 11th, Frank wrote his last letter from Camp Gordon. He writes, *"Last night we had another party here. We had half of a fried chicken and either beer or soda. For once the cooks did a good job on the chicken for it was the best I have ever tasted from an army kitchen."*

Orders for a change of station were received on April 13, 1943, and the 12th Infantry bid farewell to Camp Gordon and boarded seven trains to Fort Dix, NJ.

James 1:12, "Blessed is the man who perseveres under trial, because when he has stood the test, he will receive the crown of life that God has promised to those who love him."

"*****"

Chapter Ten

Fort Dix
April to September 1943

Fort Dix was named for Major General John Dix, who served in the War of 1812 and the Civil War. Construction started as early as 1917 and served in WWI and WWII as an army training and staging area. In March 1939, it became Fort Dix and then became a permanent Army post serving the same functions as in WWI. The facility was also the home of McGuire Army Air Base, which today is McGuire Air Force Base. The 42,000 acres, which spans 20 miles from east to west, is about 18 miles southeast of Trenton, NJ.

The 4th Division arrived at Ft Dix at 6:00 am on April 15, 1943. The April temperatures were much colder that at Camp Gordon and Frank thought they would be sleeping in tents at first, but to his delight, they were assigned to regular barracks and started right away scrubbing the floors. At first, they had to eat their meals outside since the mess hall was being repainted, but in a few days, they were eating inside. One change Frank had to adjust too was the use of cameras on base was strictly prohibited, so he considered sending his camera home. At about this time letters started showing up from a girl in Hartford, CT. It turns out that she was introduced to Frank by a letter from her cousin Al MacDonald, who was from Norwich, CT. She apparently corresponded with Frank throughout 1943 and 1944 but the two never met in person.

It turns out that Frank became quite fond of her since he kept her picture pinned on the wall in his barracks noncom sleeping quarters. In fact, a few pictures of her were found in his billfold when his personal effects were returned to his parents. Her name was Virginia (Ginnie) MacInnis, and she came from a family of three sisters and two brothers, that lived in Wethersfield, CT.

Figure 89 Virginia MacInnis

She writes in her letters to Frank about how Hartford is changing with the influx of defense workers and the growth of Bradley Air Field. In a letter dated April 15th, she wrote, *"Got your picture, not bad, not bad at all."*

Figure 90 MacInnis Family

The town closest to Ft. Dix was Wrightstown, a small town with a few houses and a few liquor stores thrown in. It was an easy walk to Wrightstown, so it became a good place to go if you didn't want to go to Trenton or New York City on a 2 or 3-day pass. The buses were crowded going to Trenton or New York, and Vic found that out when it took him four hours to get from the camp to New York City which is only 75 miles away.

Frank received a letter from Mom, dated April 20, 1943, saying she sent a box of candy for Easter. That morning they found the ground covered with snow. It was indeed a late spring in 1943. She wrote, *"Billy had his glass of milk and cookie, as usual, this afternoon and went right out to play since it warmed up quite a bit. Did you hear anything about your three-day pass? Uncle Bill and Aunt Frances are coming for Easter. Mannie Costa has to do a lot of studying at his camp in Wisconsin. He said it's 8:30 every night when they get through."*

That same day, Cpl. D. A. (Mannie) Costa sent a letter to Frank's mom from Army Air Forces, Technical Training Command, Tomah, Wisconsin. He writes, *" The training courses are pretty tough and if you fail the first time you are given only one more chance and if you fail that you are out. The housing facilities are very nice, however, with steam heat, inside bathroom, and running water, just like home."*

Frank was able to get a three-day pass to be home for Easter on April 25th. He writes on Tuesday, April 27th, 6:30 pm, *"I arrived at camp 4:30 this morning without trouble. I drove from Strasbourg to Dix myself, as the others were pretty tired. I had a few hours sleep before work today, and I guess that was sufficient, as I don't feel a bit tired. Today I had one of the fellows here that is under arrest of quarters to do my laundry. He won't be getting paid this month, so he is doing laundry to get some money."*

On April 30th, Frank received a diploma showing that he had completed the Army Ranger Course successfully. Apparently everyone in the company had to complete the course, but since they only had a few diplomas to hand out, Frank was designated to receive one. May 2, 1943, Frank, Vic, Marquis and Delybovi went to Wrightstown, which is just outside the post limits. They had a good dinner in town and then went to the movies. The weather was cold and rainy, but they were fortunate to get a ride back in a GI truck. Frank wrote, *"I don't suppose Aunt Lucy has heard any more news yet, or you would have told me. I hope she will get news Richard is safe, and I shall say prayers every night for him."* As previously written, Uncle Peter and Aunt Lucy Longhany received word on April 23rd, that Richard was missing in action somewhere at sea. There would be almost another year until February 1944 before he would be declared dead. One cannot imagine the torment that his parents went through over a one-year period not knowing if their son was living, in a German prisoner camp, or deceased. Only faith in our Lord, Jesus Christ, would have carried them through such a difficult period.

Frank would usually send home extra money to be placed in his hometown savings account. On May 4th, he sent home $50 and wrote, *"I thought I had better send it home, and you can bank it. If I kept it on me, I probably would be lending it out. Still giving instructions on rifle marksmanship. It's pretty dull work. While I was at the service club last night, I had four ice cream nut sundaes. They really are worth 15 cents because there was 15 cents worth of walnuts on them. I probably will go back for more tonight."* Now there are indeed advantages of being in the army and serving our country.

On May 15, 1943, Frank made application for an additional $5,000 of life insurance per the National Life Insurance Act of 1940 and was in addition to the $5,000 purchased in December 1941. The cost was about the same, $3.40 per month. In later years, this insurance played a role in allowing his brother Billy to enter and graduate from college with $2,500 of his funds and $2,500 of Frank's insurance funds. As fate would play out, Billy was able to obtain a college degree in place of his brother who did not have the funds to attend college after high school.

Mother's Day arrived, and Frank tried to get a three-day pass but was not successful, since he was now attending mine and demolition school and would soon be instructing others in the company. Now that he was close to Trenton and Philadelphia they would see the sights whenever they could. On May 10, 1943, he wrote, *"Yesterday Sgt. Kowalski, Bob Leonard and I decided to visit Trenton and bowled a few games. We had a nice time there together. Vic didn't go with us because he was getting a furlough today."* Camden, NJ, was also a close city to visit, which Sgt. Marquis and Frank visited on Saturday, May 16th. He writes, *"Last night we missed our bus, and since it was quite late, we took a room at a hotel here. This morning we went to church in Camden. It was the first time I believe I ever contributed to the church collection by paying as you enter. It seemed so strange. Marquis says that it is the regular practice in Rhode Island. We stayed at the USO club here, and it is a nice place. While Marquis is reading, I decided to write. There are more sailors here than soldiers. This is also true of Philadelphia."*

In the middle of May, Frank continued to give instructions to the company on anti-tank mines, mine laying, and removal. He says, *"The job was exasperating. Most of the men were interested only in catching some sleep. Last night at the service club, a soldier who can play piano very well entertained us. Mac says he used to be a concert pianist and that he played all over Europe."* Apparently back home at this time merchants were taking advantage of food shortages and were charging high prices for food products. Frank writes, *"Its too bad these merchants are in a position to take advantage of the war to do as they please. The dam chiselers. Sgt. Goldberg tells me it's almost impossible to buy potatoes in New York City. He says that they charge 25 cents a pound for potatoes. And just a few years ago farmers were only getting 20 cents per bushel."*

As May drew to an end, the training continued with the use of gas masks and simulated poison gas encounters. The marches also continued like 17 or 20 miles with a pack. The only difference at Ft Dix was that the temperatures were cooler that Georgia, which made it much easier. Frank wrote on May 26th, *"We made a 17-mile march yesterday. It was a nice day for marching, so everyone except two went all the way. Last night Mac, Vic and I walked to the old service club, which is about two miles from our barracks and found that there was a dance being held there. So we turned about and walked to the Pointville Community Center another two miles. Mac said we were like the sailor on a holiday who spent his time rowing a boat."* Well, I can't imagine marching 17 miles in the day and then in the evening walking another four miles to and from town. Now you have to be in excellent shape to accomplish that feat!

At the end of May, Frank had a portrait taken and mailed it home. He wrote on May 29th, *"The furlough I believed I was going to get next month is off. It seems that it's the policy of our company not to give furloughs during the months of July and August. So that just about leaves me flat till September. I got a good laugh out of Billy's encounter with that little bully. Tell Bill, he did right."*

Little did Frank know that he would get a furlough by mid-June.

On May 30, 1943, two soldiers from Company C were killed in an auto accident on the way back to camp. There were six riding in the car, and all were killed. Frank related the tragedy in a letter dated May 31st. *"One of those who were in the accident had been home on a pass the same time I was home. He, Vic, Husak and I took turns driving. We haven't heard any of the details of the accident, but probably the fellow driving went to sleep. One of our officers left today to identify the men."* Unfortunately, this was fairly common during the war years. These soldiers were in their late teens to their early twenties and took many chances on little sleep and many times influenced by alcohol. Cars were not as safe as now, since many of the safety features on cars today, including seat belts, had not been invented yet. Sometimes the company would be given an incentive for all to complete a long March. On June 8th, the company made a 25-mile march with light packs and when they returned they had fried chicken and beer. Now, that is an incentive! Frank writes, *"I finished the hike in good shape and that night went to the service club where a show sponsored by radio station WJZ was being held. Halfway through the show, we had an air raid alert, and that finished that. Last night I went to Wrightstown and bought a pair of dress shoes. First, however, I had*

to go to a ration board here in camp to get a ticket. What a dam joke! I had one hard time finding a pair of shoes that fit well as the stores in Wrightstown are small stores and they don't carry much stock."

In a few days, the battalion went on alert, and there was scheduled a five-day field problem. Frank heard that he had a chance for a furlough the end of June but writes, *"But don't count on it. I don't even plan on it. Since I spent about $33 this month for my uniform and shoes, I will need train fare to get home if I should happen to get a furlough. So if you can borrow $15 from Al for me and wire it to me, so I get it by next Saturday, I won't be caught short. Besides spending money for my uniform, I also lent out $10 this month, and that left my pocketbook lean. How is Bill getting along with his dog? Tell him our little dog we have here in our barracks was chewing up my shoes the other day when I came upstairs to my room."*

Figure 91 Mannie & Frank at Home

Frank did get his summer furlough on June 17th and was home for two weeks until returning on July 1st. While Frank was home, his brother-in-law, Mannie Costa was home on furlough as well. It must have been a very joyous time with all the family together, enjoying home cooked meals, drinking Dad's homemade wine and seeing relatives and friends.

105

Figure 92 Frank on Furlough

On July 1st, he writes, *"The trip back was easy and faster than I thought. It was nearly 8:00 pm when I got in New York. A train for Trenton left at 9:30 pm and I took it. There were a large number of inductees on it going to Ft Dix. It was a fast train as it only took an hour to get to Trenton. I had dinner in Trenton and took a bus for camp immediately afterward. It was about 12:30 am when I got into our company area."*

The first week of July the company spent considerable time on the firing range. For three days they were up at 4:00 am and out to the rifle range for the entire day, returning to barracks at 9:45 pm to clean rifles and then retiring by 12:00 am. The company was darn glad when that drill was over. The next day the company was put on a 16-mile march. Frank writes, *"It wasn't difficult, and everyone made it. The weather was in our favor, and the roads we took were good ones. Yesterday and the day before we had watermelon for supper. I was quite surprised. Do they still charge $2 for them at home?"* Then on July 14, 1943, he wrote, *"The fellow in my squad who I told you about being 45 is getting his discharge tomorrow. He is quite happy about it and is celebrating already. He has a job waiting for him as a brakeman on the Reading Railroad. I am glad to see him get it. He is too old for this work."*

Rifle marksmanship training continued the week of July 17th. The company with the highest points at the end of the month would be treated to a beer party, and they also will get off duty before noon on Saturdays. Company C was leading by a half of a point the week before.

Frank writes on July 17th, *"Last night I went to a show. It was a war picture and not so good. There also was a free show at the open-air theater. I wish I had gone to that one as the fellows told me that Jimmy Duranty was there in person. I got a big laugh out of Billy spraying the potato plants with water."* Frank spent the next few days at the firing range working in the pits where the targets are kept and where the scores are marked. They were up at 4:00 am and didn't quit till 8:30 pm, a real long day. On Sunday, July 25th, Vic and Frank visited Sgt. DeLybovi at the hospital. He was their platoon sergeant and had been in the hospital for about two weeks. He apparently contracted malaria while he was in Hawaii and has not felt good since. The last week of July, Eleanor and Mary made a trip to Richmond, VA, where Eleanor's husband, Mannie Costa, was now stationed.

On July 31, 1943, the regimental commander informed the troops that the 4th Division would lose their half-tracs and become a triangular infantry division. Mac said, *"So they will have to change our name from the rolling 4th to the strolling 4th!"* It's interesting that this change was made, and one wonders what politics entered into this decision. The author is undoubtedly not an expert on military strategy but when the 4th was first in combat on D-Day, and afterward, the infantry had little cover and suffered heavy losses, that possibly could have been reduced with mechanized equipment. Colonel Gerden Johnson writes in his book, History of the 12th Infantry Regiment in WWII, *"...the departure from Ft Dix was not without a note of sadness for the War Department had decided to de-motorize the 4th Division. The shock action, mobility and sustained firepower which denoted the division's tactics, symbolized the tough fighting spirit and hard hitting team which every individual felt he was a part of, and the loss of our motorized equipment was akin to the Cavalryman's loss of his horse. Hence fourth "Joe" was to become known more and more as the foot-*

slogging "Dough" as the Fourth Motorized Division became once more known as the 4th Infantry Division." (2)

Figure 79 1st Battalion Company C

Frank wrote August 8, 1943, that Company C was going to change commanders again. Capt. Stoneman was leaving, and this would make the fourth commander they have had in the past two years. Frank received a card from his sister Mary from Richmond, VA that she and Eleanor were seeing Mannie Costa, who was now stationed there. When they arrived at the base, they found Mannie marching on the drill field. When the drill sergeant saw Eleanor and Mary watching, he inquired whom they wanted to see. When they gave Pvt. Mannie Costa's name, Mannie was so thrilled that he left rank and started over to see them. Immediately the drill sergeant gave the order for Mannie to get back in rank, which caused the men to start laughing. The sergeant, himself amused said, "If that is your wife, you better break rank and start taking orders from her".

The week of August 10th saw more combat range firing. The drill was up at 4:30 am, have breakfast and then head to the range. There was a new course for rifle firing, and everyone was required to make a qualifying score of eight. Many men did not qualify, but Frank did with a score of 15 points first time up. He was becoming an excellent marksman. It was a long day being 9:00 pm before returning to barracks. Then two hours to clean rifles.

Frank wrote on August 15th, *"Today I visited Philadelphia, had dinner there and then went to a show. I went alone. Consequently, I didn't have as good a time as if I had been with someone. I just received our company's picture, and I will mail it tomorrow. I am in the back row, and if my memory is correct, I am ninth left of the flag. Since this is a motorized company, all the equipment is shown in the background. One of the men in our company had some real bad luck on Friday the 13th. He was on guard and went to sleep on his post. The officer of the guard found him sleeping and took his rifle away then woke him and put him under arrest. This fellow is in great danger of getting a very stiff sentence. Sleeping on guard duty is one of the worst offenses a soldier can commit in the eyes of the army. I hope they don't go to hard on him as he is a nice fellow."*

The last week of August, Frank was again on the firing range coaching the men for qualification. It made for a long day since you were up at 4:00 am and did not return to barracks until 9:00 pm. On August 26th a soldier was killed when he stood up in the scoring pit, exposing himself to fire and was shot through the face. How unfortunate such accidents occur during training. At this time Frank's squad was turned over to Sgt. Richardson and Frank was given the post of platoon guide. Vic Santangelo was promoted to platoon sergeant as Sgt. Delybove was given a medical discharge. Sgt. Richardson now shared a room with Frank and turned out to be a natural born comedian, always keeping everyone around in laughs.

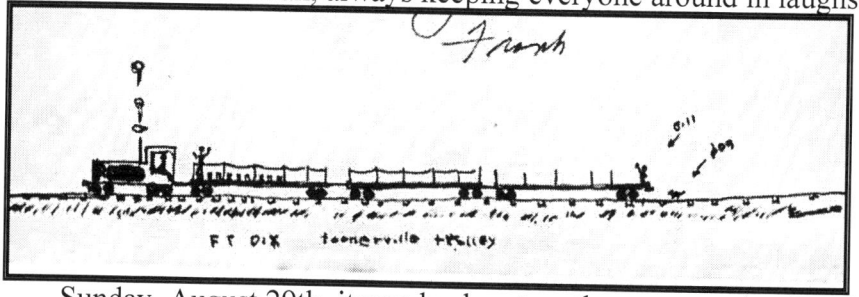

Sunday, August 29th, it was back out on the range again. Frank wrote, *"We went out to the range on the little Toonervillle trolley, and we got the biggest laugh of the day when the engine and a couple of cars ahead of us uncoupled and pulled away from our car. The engineer was about 300 yards away from us before he found out he had lost some cars. In the trip out I saw four deer running through the fields. There seems to be quite a few up here on the reservation."*

It was about this time that the 12th Regiment did its part in helping out in a severe crisis that was threatening the tomato crop in New Jersey. There was a critical shortage of labor and thousands of tons of tomatoes on several hundred trucks stood unloaded at the Campbell Soup Company's plant in Camden, NJ. The Federal government ordered troops from Ft Dix and infantrymen performed a valuable service in unloading trucks and processing tomatoes. The soldiers were transported to and from the plant and while there were fed and housed in the Campbell Soup Plant. Frank did not mention this in his letters so maybe he did not participate. (2)

Frank was on a three-day problem Thursday, September 2nd, during which it was hot, and the men drank all their water from their canteens. After Frank got back and cleaned up, he went to the service club, had supper, and then had three glasses of iced tea, four root beers, and finally two sundaes. He wrote, *"Then I felt much better!"* Saturday afternoon, September 4, 1943, Frank and

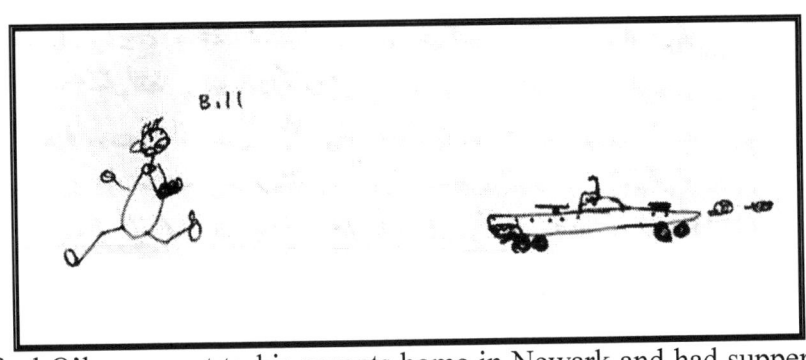

Alfred O'hern, went to his parents home in Newark and had supper. Afterward, they left for Coney Island and being late when they got there they found the park blacked out, but there still was quite a crowd. No doubt a blackout was necessary since they were on the Atlantic coastline and German subs were patrolling offshore. On September 8th, Frank received a surprise letter from a hometown friend, Bill Morgan. Apparently he was stationed on an island in the Pacific. Morgan writes, *"I wish I were back in the states as the new general we have is trying to stop all the beer that comes on the island."* Now, what do you think his chances were of accomplishing that feat? If he did, he would have a mutiny.

The early part of September, rumors were flying that there was going to be another change of station somewhere to the South. They were ordered to clean their barracks again since they had to be spotless before leaving. The fellows were joking about the strict cleaning and inspections. Some were saying that the insignia should be crossed mops instead of rifles, and the only reason they were going to another camp is that the next camp needed a cleaning. So naturally they would send them. It was now certain that the 4th Division was moving to a new destination. Frank wrote on September 13th, *"Very soon now I will be leaving here. We already know our destination, and I can safely say that this other camp is farther south than the other one we were in before. Not many of the men like the prospects of going south again, but it will be a good place to spend the winter. We are to get a new type of training down there. Just got back from Wrightstown where I bought a pair of swimming trunks. According to the latest dope, there will be opportunities for salt water swimming at the new camp."*

Frank received a letter from home on September 17th saying that they already had a frost at home. Uncle Bill and Aunt Fran were moving again which was not much of a surprise since they were always moving from one city to another. Uncle Bill was a salesman for the Todd Company which made check writers office equipment.

The new type of training for the next move would be in the use of landing craft on beachheads and was to be held at Camp Gordon Johnston in the panhandle of Florida. On Monday, September 20th, Frank wrote that they would be moving real soon. The trip would take about three days. He wrote, *"It has been quite cold here at Dix the past week. I picked up a darn cold, and that is something unusual for me. Possibly because I didn't dress warmly enough or maybe, it was the quick change in the weather. Sunday afternoon Bob Leonard, Sgt. Kozlowski and I decided to go to New York City. We had a good time, and we caught the last train back to camp. It was late when we reached camp, and we had to walk from the bus station to the barracks a distance of 2 miles at least."*

The next day Frank had bad news about Sgt. Marquis who sleeps in his room. He was absent for two days. Frank wrote, *"Its too bad he let the booze and women get the best of him. He will be reduced to a private when he comes back, and he will be lucky if he doesn't get the guard house."*

"Romans 8:28 "We know that in all things God works for the good of those who love him, who have been called according to his purpose."

"*****"

Chapter Eleven

Camp Gordon Johnston
September to November 1943

Amphibious operations before WWII had been limited in scope and were confined to river crossings or small raids on enemy-held shores. Operations on such a grand scale were not anticipated at the start of WWII. It was apparent that the United States did not have sufficient troops trained for this type of operation, which was now required to win the war. A study of amphibious forces in a paper prepared by the Joint US Staff Planners in April 1942 recognized that it would be impractical to have Marine troops undertake all amphibious operations because sufficient Marine troops would not be available. The Army was trained and organized for ground infantry warfare and had sufficient troops available for amphibious training. The study showed that the structure of amphibious training at the time was unwieldy, ineffective and dangerous. The recommendation was made and accepted that the Army be charged with the planning, preparation and training for large scale amphibious operations and the Navy and the Marine Corps assist the Army with equipment, technical advice, and cooperation.

At this time, a tactical plan, the XXX Plan, was under consideration that involved scores of troops who were to be employed in a large amphibious operation. Every division earmarked for employment under the XXX Plan were to receive complete shore to shore amphibious training, and the objective was to train twelve divisions by February 1, 1943. On May 9, 1942, the plan was to train four divisions at Camp Edwards, MA, six divisions at Caravelle, FL, and two at Fort Lewis, WA. To fulfill this mission, the Army activated the Amphibious Training Center on May 20, 1942. The training for Camp Gordon Johnston was very extensive, which included several types of training. Boat training covered the loading and unloading of landing craft quickly and quietly by day or night, boat discipline, boat formations and control of landing craft, organization and control of troops during loading and unloading operations, and tactical operation and supply of combat teams.

Figure 94 Amphibious Landing at Camp Gordon Johnston

Beach training included the seizure of the beachhead, crossing beach obstacles and defensive works, clearing the beach of obstacles, and subsequent beach organization. Training for support operations included resupply, night operations, development of an intelligence system for amphibious operations, development of a signal communication system, the use of smoke for screening, the use of chemicals for contamination, and methods of decontamination. Air operation training included air-ground support and anti-aircraft defense. Soldier training covered swimming, camouflage, knife and bayonet fighting, judo, infiltration, the battle firing of automatic weapons from landing craft and combat in cities. This training task was overwhelming but at the same time necessary for a successful military operation to invade a foreign shore.

The Army closed the Amphibious Training Center in March 1943 after operating for over a year and training several combat groups. Its personnel were scattered to the four winds except the 75th Composite Infantry Training Battalion. It was retained for the conduct of further amphibious training under the supervision of the Navy who was now directed to have the prime responsibility. Then on September 7, 1943, the battalion was ordered to Camp Gordon Johnston to reopen the camp for the training of the 4th Infantry Division in ship to shore operations under the supervision of the Navy. Training started on October 1, 1943, and ran until November 30th at which time the camp was again closed as far as amphibious training was concerned. (2)

On September 25, 1943, the 4th Division reached Camp Gordon Johnston in Florida for amphibious training. First, there were two weeks of school, which was followed by training in landing craft of the 4th Engineer Special Brigade. The men endured their first seasickness, and they made assault landings on Dog Island and the local beach. Night marches were now the norm to avoid the Florida heat, and it brought some compensation by swimming in the afternoon in the Gulf of Mexico. Since many men did not know how to swim or were weak swimmers, in the months of October and November emphasis was placed on swimming instructions to enable them to survive the waters when abandoning ship. At this time, there was a change in officer personnel. Lt. Col. James S. Luckett, Lt. Col. John W. Merrill and Lt. Col. Thaddeus Dulin joined the 4th Division and were assigned to the 12th Infantry. (3)

Frank wrote on September 25, 1943, *"At about 8:00 pm, I reached our new camp, Gordon Johnston, FL. The nearest city to the camp is Tallahassee, and that's about fifty miles from here. We are on the Gulf of Mexico. Our trip was a good one. We left Ft Dix 1:00 am Wednesday. We traveled in Pullman cars, and I had an upper berth and slept well both nights. It is very warm here. Our barracks have no floors. Just sand. There is a theater and an exchange nearby."* Next day the 26th, Saturday, he writes, *"We have quite a bit of work ahead of us today till we get settled. I just set my radio up, and I can get one station on it. Despite the poor barracks and facilities down here I think I will have some fun. I will get a chance to do all the swimming I want."*

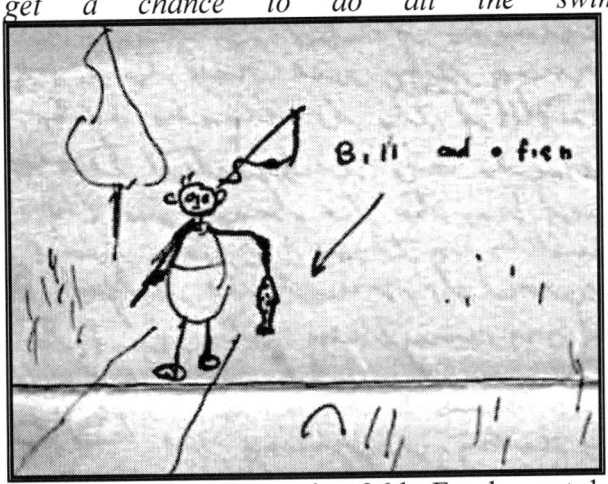

On Sunday, September 26th, Frank went down to the beach and swam in the warm water most of the afternoon. Several men went shore casting and saw fish that they had never seen before. Birmingham caught a fish and after pulling it out of the water, it blew itself up, until it was like a little balloon. Vic, Marquis, Richardson, and Frank went to the theater for the first time, which was an open-air type. They waited until after dark and the place never opened up. They were indeed darn angry for wasting the whole night for nothing. Soon they found the chapel, but it was an open-air type as well. This camp was sure different and seemed primitive compared to the previous ones. They may not have realized that most of the camp was closed in March 1943 and then was reduced in size and function. Some of Frank's friends, wanting to see the big city, went to Tallahassee right away and reported back that it wasn't much of a town. There was a curfew in effect at 10:30 every night. Rumors started soon that they would only be there for six weeks with only two weeks of amphibious training and the rest spent in preparation for the ship-to-shore operations. They were informed that all men would be required to swim a minimum of 25 yards.

On Sunday, September 27, 1943, Frank went swimming most of the afternoon. He went to the theater that evening and saw the movie, "This Is The Army." He said, *"I didn't like this picture probably because I've enough army around me all day without seeing soldiers in the movies."* During the war period, Hollywood mostly produced war-themed movies primarily to develop the morale of the country. The men started right away to work on their primitive barracks by building some clothes racks and putting in double decker beds to replace the folding cots. Frank went swimming ever chance he could and one afternoon saw a small shark that had been left on the beach. Someone had cut a chunk out of its side and probably was going to try shark steak. That evening there were more fishermen than you could count on the pier and some were getting some good-sized fish. That would have been an excellent addition to the standard army chow. At this time, men started to get furloughs, but Frank didn't think he would be in the first group. He realized that a furlough from Camp Gordon Johnston was not that great since he would spend half of his time going to and from his home in New York State.

Frank soon found out that the use of cameras on the post was very limited. Certain areas and equipment were not allowed to be photographed. Frank had planned to take pictures of the boats they would use for training, but now that's out. On September 30, 1943, the night marches began, starting at 8:00 pm and returning the next day at 4:30 am. Much better to march at night, though, since it is much cooler. The next day Frank was in charge of his platoon since

Vic was on furlough. Vic was now going to make Staff Sergeant, which would be a great help to him since he had plans to get married soon.

Sunday, October 3, 1943, Frank was back swimming in the ocean again and when he was ready to leave he watched some airplanes bombing some targets on an island out in the bay. He wrote, *"They sure put on quite a show."* The next day he received a box of cookies from home and mom wrote that they had a good crop of potatoes, which should bring in a good price.

On October 5th, they had a 15-mile march, which Frank says was a cinch as far as marches go. It was warm out, but there was a cool ocean breeze blowing all day, which was a great help. Frank writes, *"Someone brought Marquis two beers from the PX, and he gave me one. It was pretty good, as I was feeling thirsty. Unfortunately Sgt. Marquis was reduced in grade because he was absent two days the previous month, but the good news is that he won't be punished further. It turns out that those days he was absent, he was on his honeymoon. While on a three-day pass he decided all at once to get married but if he had used his head he could have got another pass instead of going off without permission."* Now how could we expect him use his head since he was in love!

Many rumors were now flying about concerning the upcoming training. One rumor was that half of the 8th Infantry had contracted malaria on Dog Island. However, Frank found out that the 8th Infantry had not been over to the island yet, so that quashed that rumor. Frank now wanted to get a pass to Tallahassee and see the sights even if it had the reputation of a small town where the sidewalks were rolled up at night. There was a convoy going to Ocala Springs where he heard the water is so clear you can see anything at the bottom, but circumstances prevented him from going. At this time, Frank got some disconcerting news from home that Eleanor had not heard from her husband Mannie Costa in a few weeks. That was a sure indication that he had most likely been deployed overseas. What a concern and worry that must have been for his sister Eleanor.

On Saturday Frank started the day with a good swim in the Gulf of Mexico and that night went to Tallahassee with Sgt. Marquis. He was impressed with Tallahassee since it was clean and not very large which suited him just fine. He bought a souvenir to send back home and after got a ride with a soldier who had his car at camp. During the trip, Frank was surprised to see cows wandering freely alongside and across the road and knew it would be very dangerous to drive fast at night in this part of Florida. Evidently the farmers have free range and don't use fences in that part of the state. On Sunday afternoon, he went for a swim again at the beach and then went to a movie that night and saw "Thank Your Lucky Stars" which he recommended that the family see back home.

On October 13th, they had another 25-mile march, which was held again at night due to some warm weather. However, on October 16th, a real cold wind came in, and Frank canceled his plans for another swim. He wrote, *"Sgt. Goldberg's mother died yesterday, and the men in the company took up a collection so he could fly home to NYC. He has had some hard luck. His brother was shot down in an air raid just about a month ago. I went to the main PX last night and then to the service club where a dance was being held. The main PX is better than ours, but it is ten miles from here. The only way to get there is by bus and the bus service in this camp isn't so good."* Isn't it remarkable how these soldiers would help each other in times of adversity like the death of a loved one back home? That says a lot for our soldiers back then who cared for each other's welfare during a trying period in our history.

On October 11th, Frank heard that Mannie was now somewhere in England. Mannie wrote to Frank's brother, Billy, that he was now doing the work he was trained for and getting along well. On their time off they had bicycles that they could ride in the English countryside and see nearby towns. He could not write about where he was or what towns he visited since all letters were censored. After the war we found out he was in radio communications, the 57th Fighter Control Center, to talk the Army Air Force pilots back to England after their missions over Europe. His job was not without danger, however, as one day a German Buzz Bomb crashed and exploded very close to their radio communication tower and the force of the explosion knocked him off his stool. He wrote, *"I am doing my part to help get rid of the Germans so we all can get back home and live in peace once again."* Yes, that is indeed the prayer of many soldiers and the families back home in a terrible world war!

Frank continued to get new training at the camp but was never specific as to the nature of it probably because they were told not to reveal details. He did often say that they would have night problems and 15 to 25-mile marches were common. Then in early October, the training turned to the LCVP (Landing Craft Vehicle Personnel), more commonly called Higgins Boats. On October 26th, he writes, *"We had been out all day since 3:00 am on a problem and then at midnight last night we were out again. We were out in the boats from 2:00 am till 10:30 am. It was quite a ride as the water was a little rough and it came flying over the bow into the boat not infrequently. I kept pretty dry as I covered myself with a raincoat. One of the fellows in the boat got very sick from the rocking of the boat. I didn't have any trouble, though, in fact, I haven't been seasick any time we have been out. Our landing craft couldn't make it all the way to the shore, so we had about 25 yards to wade before reaching the beach. The problem ended early in the afternoon, and we got rides back to the barracks in trucks. I wish I could have taken movies of the flotilla of boats. It would have been something to show on a screen especially in color, but that is not permitted. Today's problem finished up our phase of the amphibious training. We have, however, a sort of an exhibition for the benefit of the civilians."*

Figure 95 Landing with Higgins Boats

Now, Frank was a little disappointed in the ice cream at the PX and by now we know how much he liked the stuff. He writes, *"The* ice cream we get at the PX is half sherbet. We can get good ice cream at the main PX, but that's ten miles away, so I don't go up there very often though there are truck taxies that go there from our area. I saw that picture you mentioned a few weeks ago, and I didn't think it was anything extra. One of the actors in it used to be in Cannon Company of our regiment. He was a supply sergeant in the supply room next to our own. In the picture, he does some tap dancing and some aerobatics."

Frank noted that they got a new company commander on November 3, 1943, replacing a commander they only had four months. He still had the hope of a furlough soon and saw Mac go home on Monday. Frank wrote, *"I talked with a fellow who went home by plane a few weeks ago on an emergency furlough. It cost him $43 from Jacksonville to NY, and he had to show the emergency furlough to get a plane. I can get home in two days or less by train as there are some fast trains that leave Jacksonville for NY."*

Frank was not a smoker, and the only alcohol he drank was an occasional beer. He wrote on November 3rd, *"Yesterday I was coaching on the grenade course, and I'm glad that's over with. We had a beer party here tonight, but I kept away. It usually ends in a fight. As it was, I steered a couple of boys away from there back to the barracks. They were in a quarrel and ready to fight. Some of those guys get a few beers in them and want to whip the whole world."* It may have been at this time that he had a very close call when instructing on the range. A soldier he was instructing on grenades panicked when he was getting ready to throw the grenade after pulling the pin. The grenade slipped out of his hand and fell to the ground a few feet from them. Frank and the soldier dove into a pit just before it went off. That was indeed a close call for both of them. He did not tell his parents because he did not want to alarm them, but they later found out from one of his buddies.

Night marches continued well into November. Frank wrote November 8th, *"We were on a nine-mile cross-country hike this afternoon, but it was a cinch. Nine miles is just a stroll for us now. Thursday night we have a 25 miler. A 25-mile march doesn't bother me much except I am a little tired after I finish it. Marching at night is a hundred percent easier than in the daytime. A full field pack isn't so bad if you know how to make one properly. Once the straps are adjusted right, there isn't any strain on it, and I've had plenty of practice in adjusting them."*

Frank got his furlough on November 13, 1943, for 14 days and arrived back at camp around 9:00 pm Friday, the 27th. Thanksgiving was on November 25th, so he was able to spend Thanksgiving Day with the family and left the next morning very early by train. The visit with the family was the last time they would see him alive.

The storm clouds were building fast for an invasion of Europe and where Frank would play a vital role as part of the 12th Regiment, 4th Division. Many men went home that Thanksgiving and Christmas in 1943 never to return. Yes, war indeed is a terrible scar on humanity. Frank wrote on November 27th, *"The trip down was okay, and I had a seat all the way. I was in Tallahassee yesterday afternoon at 3:00 pm but had to wait till 7:00 pm for the bus to camp. I was lucky to get on this bus as it was very crowded. This afternoon our company is having their Thanksgiving dinner. They were out on a problem Thursday, so they are having it today. So I will have another Thanksgiving dinner!"*

Two days later, November 29th, the 4th Division left Camp Gordon Johnston. Further information on Camp Gordon Johnston can be obtained from the web site, http://www.campgordonjohnston.com and on Facebook, Camp Gordon Johnston Museum.

Psalm 37:5-6, "Commit your way to the Lord; trust in him and he will do this: He will make your righteousness shine like the dawn."

"****"

Chapter Twelve

Fort Jackson
November 1943 to January 1944

In early December 1943, the regiment was moved to Fort Jackson, SC, which is just outside Columbia, S.C. The officers and men that had not received furloughs for six months or more were allowed to take leave. The training had now advanced to the point where weapons firing had been completed to where every man was familiar with all weapons in his unit. Consequently, the Army and War Department inspectors were all over the regiment, conducting inspections, reviewing records and ordering physical examinations. At this time equipment was packed and boxed according to secret instructions. By mid-December Major Kenneth E. Lay, Capt. James P. Smith and Lt. Rudolph Walters left Ft. Jackson as an advance party headed for an unknown secret destination. As of midnight December 26, 1943, the 12th Infantry was alerted for overseas movement.

The 12th Regiment left Camp Gordon Johnston by rail around 9:00 am on November 29, 1943, and at 12:30 pm they were in Ft. Jackson, S.C. Shortly after arrival Frank wrote, *"This looks like a swell camp. There is good bus service to Columbia. We are near the church, the service club, Post Exchange, theater, cleaners, barbershop and the bowling alleys. Our barracks are small, housing fifteen men in each. There are two stoves in each barrack, and our kitchen is quite a change from Gordon Johnston. It is a big mess hall, and we have tables and plates and cups. All in all, I think I will like this camp, it sure is quite a change from our old one."* Little did Frank know that they would only spend a few weeks at Ft. Jackson before deployment overseas?

On the trip to Ft. Jackson, Frank had Sgt. Richardson pack his radio in his footlocker. On arrival at Jackson, Frank found a hole punched in the speaker. He patched it with some scotch tape, and it played as good as ever and discovered much to his delight that there were several radio stations nearby. December 3, 1943, was payday, and the men would be crowding the streets of Columbia for restaurants and bars. Frank was ordered to report to the medics in the afternoon with a detail of men to check on their eyeglasses. There was a need for a final check to ensure the men that needed glasses were properly fit for duty for the upcoming deployment.

Frank wrote, *"Al MacDonald's brother was missing in action for seven weeks. His mother just received word that he was safe."* It was sure good to hear news such as this since there was so much bad news every week. On Sunday, December 5th, Frank and Mac took a trip to Greenwood, SC, a town about 75 miles from Columbia. They had been there once before when they were on maneuvers last spring. Mac knew some people there who were related to a friend of his in Connecticut. It was about 9:30 pm before they got back to Columbia and found a good restaurant to have a swell southern fried chicken dinner. The training at camp was light so far. At this time, Frank had been in eight different camps over the past two and half years. He wrote his sister Mary, *"Golly I'm getting to be a regular vagabond. This place (Ft Jackson) is a H--l of a lot different from the one we left. We have good barracks, a mess hall with china, a PX with barbers and tailors, a theater with a roof and even a bowling alley. The chow here is even better. For instance, yesterday we had fried chicken and today we had steak. Doesn't that make you hungry? Columbia, the capital of SC, is only seven miles from camp, a ten-minute bus ride. It is quite a good size city, but it is pretty well crowded with GIs. Yesterday Mac and I took a bus to Greenwood, SC. We had been there once before on maneuvers. Our original idea was to go somewhere where there weren't many soldiers. HA! When we arrived in Greenwood half of the 4th Division was there before us."*

The training continued to be on the light side and seemed almost like a vacation to the men. The morning of December 8th there was a five-mile speed March, and they did it in nothing flat. Frank for the first time received a letter from his youngest brother, Billy, who was seven years old. Frank says, *"He writes very well for his first letter. I will send him a letter soon."* At about this time a flu epidemic was spreading throughout the country. Frank was concerned about his family back home and cautioned them if they get a cold it is best not to take chances but to get to bed and much rest. Frank wrote on December 15th, *"The weather has changed considerably here in the past two days. Last night it rained and today it's snowing. One of the fellows from our platoon whose home is in SC tells me that this is the first time it has snowed here in seven years. Many of the boys are trying to get passes over the Christmas holiday. An order just came down, however, curtailing all passes because of the flu epidemic. It's a tough order for the men who live a short distance from the camp as they could get home easily over the weekend. I don't think we will remain at this camp all winter. And if we should leave there's always the possibility it may be nearer home."* Well as fate would have it, this would not be the case since plans were already made for overseas deployment in early January 1944.

Frank got some good news on December 19th from the local paper. In the paper, there was an article about the army stating that in all qualified infantry units, all platoon sergeants will be advanced one grade to technical sergeants and platoon guides will be made staff sergeants. If this were to go through, Frank would become staff sergeant and draw $96 per month, an $18 increase a month. Frank got another pleasant surprise December 21st when he received a letter from the Jell-O Company notifying him that they were giving him a bond for Christmas and a bonus of $25. Frank would send the money home for his saving account so he would be able to go back to school after the war. However as fate would have it, this would not happen.

Christmas 1943 arrived, and the boys at Ft Jackson were doing their best to celebrate the holiday at camp.

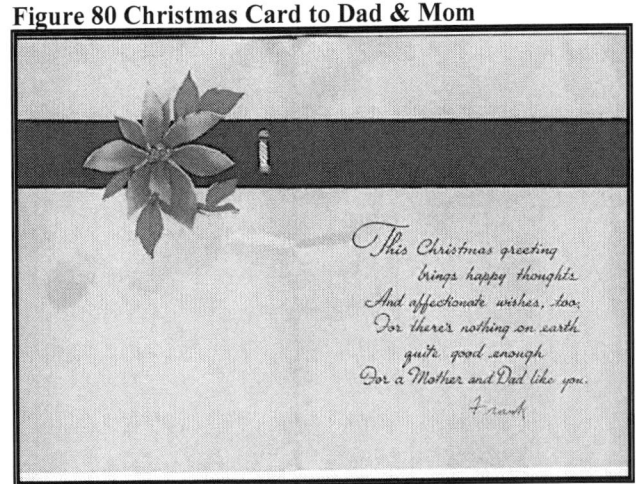

Figure 80 Christmas Card to Dad & Mom

Figure 97 Christmas Card to Eleanor

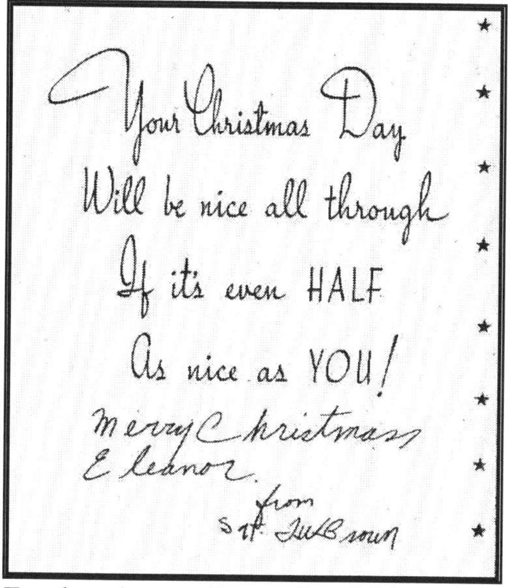

> Your Christmas Day
> Will be nice all through
> If it's even HALF
> As nice as YOU!
> Merry Christmas
> Eleanor
> from
> S/Sgt. Jul Brown

Frank writes on December 24th, *"It's Christmas Eve once more and here in camp its pretty quiet. I just put some more coal in our little stove, and the fire is going full blast. Outside the air is very sharp but it's nice and cozy in here. The shelf above my bed is decorated with some real holly that Vic got out in the woods. He couldn't get any mistletoe although there is a lot of it around this part of the country. We also hung a little bell by the door and when anyone comes in it rings like the dickens. Then we shout Merry Christmas. We have more fun with that than a bunch of kids. I bet Billy is all excited and can't wait till he opens his presents. Ha! Tomorrow we are having a big turkey dinner. The mess hall is all decorated, and it looks pretty good. My radio is in fine shape tonight, and the Christmas carols are coming over quite regular."*

Merry Christmas Frank and all the men and women scattered across the globe fighting this horrific, terrible war. Our most gracious God blessed all of you in 1943 and comforted your families back home.

On December 29th, Frank wrote, *"Today the company commander told us about the new promotions I wrote about. I don't know when we will get them, but I guess it's pretty certain we will get them."* Frank due to secrecy could not write home at this time, that at midnight, December 26th, the 12th Infantry was alerted for overseas movement. It would not be long now, and they would be crossing the Atlantic to prepare for the Normandy invasion.

On January 1, 1944, Frank and Mac on a warm sunny afternoon went to Rock Hill; a small town about a three-hour ride from

125

Columbia. They had a good turkey dinner for only 60 cents, but it must have been his off day because he lost one of his gloves and his bus ticket. Then Mac discovered he lost his bus ticket as well. At this time, Frank shipped his suitcase with extra khaki and wool clothing home since they were not allowed to keep extra clothing. It was probably in preparation for the overseas deployment. Then on Saturday, the company commander called the noncoms to inform them that the promotions were going through. Platoon guides weren't listed for promotions so the company commander changed platoon guides to squad leaders so they could get the rating. Frank was now promoted to staff sergeant and would draw $96 per month.

The first week of January the boys were kept very busy preparing for overseas deployment, but Frank could not write home about it. He wrote on January 8th, *"I haven't had much time for writing this week as I have been quite busy. I received the box of candy, and it was darn good. Alfred's letter also arrived the same day with $20 in it. That was quite a bit. He shouldn't have sent so much as he doesn't earn too much. The night before last Vic, Mac and I went to Columbia. We had a chicken dinner, but the chicken wasn't as good as the kind we used to have in Augusta. We had some more fun with that bell again. I tied it to Kollars bedspring, and when he came in late one night and climbed into bed, it began to ring. Was he mad!"*

On January 11th, Frank wrote home that his address was again changing and to use the one on the envelope. He could not write that on that day they were starting to leave Fort Jackson for Camp Kilmer, NJ. He did write, *"Your letters arrived yesterday. I also received the box of candy that Aunt Mary sent. It was in good shape despite the distance it traveled before it reached me. We may leave this camp soon. So if there should be a time when you don't receive any letters from me it's because I'm too busy to write. As soon as I get settled, I'll write. Our mail is censored now. Too many unauthorized persons in the past always learned where we were going and when we were going. Today while playing football my watch fell to the ground in three pieces, case, works, and strap. Luckily no one stepped on them, and nothing was broken. The next time I will be more careful."*

The next two letters Frank wrote from Camp Kilmer, NJ, a staging area for military embarkation about 22 miles from New York City.

Figure 98 Frank's Change of Address Card

```
                    NOTICE OF CHANGE OF ADDRESS
      (A sufficient number of these cards will be distributed to each soldier when his mail
      address is changed to permit him to send one to each of his regular correspondents.)
                                    Date................., 1943..
   This is to advise you that my correct address now is
      Sgt          Frank W. Brown                    32181552
      (Grade)              (Name)                  (Army Serial No.) 4th
      Company "G"                          12th Infantry Div
      (Company or comparable unit)         (Regiment or comparable unit)
      APO No................  % Postmaster.................................
          (Strike out if not applicable)              (Name of post office)
                    Signature  Frank W. Brown
   NOTE.—Newspapers and magazines may need your old address for correct processing.
   My old address was......Company "G" 12th Infantry
                           Fort Jackson, S.C.

   W. D., A. G. O. Form No. 204
        April 8, 1943                                    16-33987-1   GPO
```

His letters did not reveal his location so back home it appeared he was still at Ft Jackson. The camp was activated in June 1942 as a staging area and part of the New York Port of Embarkation. The camp was organized as part of the Army Forces Transportation Corps. Troops were quartered at Camp Kilmer in preparation for transport to the European Theater of Operations. It became the largest processing center for troops heading overseas and returning from WWII, processing over 2.5 million soldiers. It officially closed in 2009. (4)

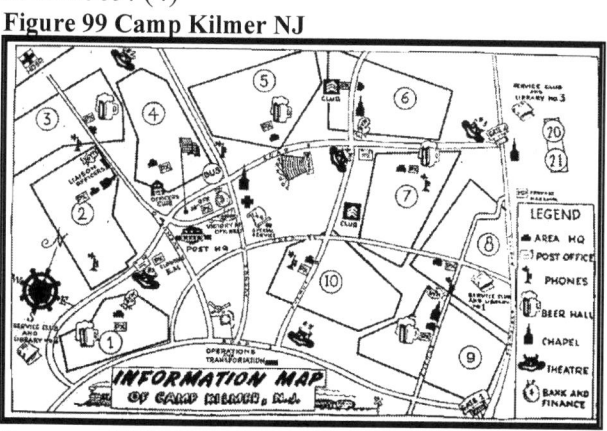

Figure 99 Camp Kilmer NJ

January 13th - *"Last night Mac and I went to a show here in camp. There was a double feature playing, and both pictures were fairly good. Bob Leonard wanted me to go to town with him tomorrow. I would like to go in, but my uniform is in the cleaners. I suppose Billy still has a lot of fun with Pal. Is he training him yet or has he given that up as a hopeless task? One of the men in our company had a pig that he was raising. He finally had to get rid of it, so some of the fellows had barbecued pork. However, this fellow*

Figure 100 Camp Kilmer

wouldn't eat it because the pig was his pet. We probably will have athletics this afternoon, so I better sign off now before we fall out."

January 14th - *"Last night after supper I went to the service club. The Song Spinners were there entertaining the soldiers. Perhaps you have seen them on the screen or heard them on the radio. They put on a pretty nice show. Enclosed in this letter you will find two cards with instructions for obtaining army emergency relief. Keep them somewhere, as they might be useful sometime. Yesterday I also made out an allotment for $25. With the increase in my pay, I can easily afford it. If I didn't make out the allotment, I would only spend the extra money, or someone would borrow it. This way I may save some and then also you would have some extra income if you need it."*

January 17th - *"Saturday I was sergeant of the guard. Didn't find much time for writing this week. Last night I went to a show in camp with Vic, Mac, and Leonard. The picture was rather good, but we had a difficult time getting in the theater. A whole mob tried to get in all at once and in the crush, someone broke a window in one of the doors. Sometimes these men are just like a bunch of cattle."*

On January 17, 1944, Frank wrote his last letter from Camp Kilmer or the states as on that day they left Camp Kilmer for an overseas transport.

John 14:27, "Peace I leave with you; my peace I give you. I do not give to you as the world gives. Do not let your hearts be troubled and do not be afraid."

"*****"

Chapter Thirteen

England
January to June 1944

On January 11, 1944, the 12 Infantry Regiment, composed of 176 officers and 3652 enlisted men, completed a rail movement from Fort Jackson, SC to Camp Kilmer, NJ, a staging area for the New York Port of Embarkation. At this time, the regiment was at its greatest strength in history. At Camp Kilmer, port officers took over and started the processing procedure. Each soldier received a final physical examination, and each item of personal and organizational equipment was inspected for service. The men received lectures on military secrecy, and final disposition of individual articles was made. Also, instructions for entrainment were given, and numbers corresponding to positions on the ship's roster were chalked on the front of steel helmets. Changes of address cards were mailed, and officers and their men were released on twelve-hour passes to New Brunswick, Trenton, and New York. At this point, the 12th Infantry was known as "Shipment 1589-G."

At 8:00 am on January 15th, the regiment was alerted and on the 17th, at 8:00 am, the regiment moved out of the Pennsylvania Railroad Yard at Camp Kilmer for the Jersey City Terminal. The regiment was then put aboard ferries and sealed, so the direction and destination were unknown. The tip of Manhattan was rounded, and they moved slowly to Pier 5 of the Brooklyn Army Base. The Brooklyn Chapter of the American Red Cross was present in the long cold, dingy pier shed, to provide lines of waiting men with hot coffee, doughnuts, and candy. Then what followed was the procedure for embarking on the ship, the US Army Transport George Washington. An officer at the gangplank would call out a soldier's name, and the soldier would reply by giving his first name and middle initial. The officer would check the roster and wave the soldier up. All through the night the process continued while the men below moved to their assigned quarters. The George

Washington became the home of the 12th Infantry for the next twelve days.

Figure 101 SS George Washington

The George Washington was commissioned in 1908 in Stettin, Germany. The North German Lloyd Line previously operated the ship as a luxury liner. It is interesting that the Germans had put a two and one-half inch nickel steel hull on her so that she could be converted into a cruiser when WWI broke out, but she was captured early in the war and held at Hoboken, NJ in 1914. The United States entered the war in 1917, and she was converted into a troop ship. At the close of WWI, she became a permanent possession of the United States and again refitted and pressed into service as a luxury liner operation for about ten years. At the beginning of WWII, she was brought into service again as a troop carrier. Before the 12th Infantry boarded the George Washington, she had completed a trip of 96 days from San Francisco to Australia, to India and around the Cape of Good Hope to New York. Now by coincidence in 1944, the regimental commander, Col. Harry M. Henderson of San Antonio, TX, who previously sailed on her on a mission to France in 1917, sailed on her again. She was a large ship, 755 ft in length with a gross tonnage of 23788 and had the largest twin up and down engines in the world. Each engine produced 11000 HP and had the largest boilers afloat. She was the greatest ship in the Army Transport Service.

In a blanket of fog at 10:00 am on January 18, 1944, the George Washington left her berth and passed through the Narrows and out to sea. At sundown, she took her place in a large convoy and was completely blacked out. A soldier's time aboard the ship followed a pattern of breakfast, calisthenics on the open decks, boat drills, ship inspections, policing and entertainment. Much time was spent guessing the final destination. Later the men found out, that the ship providing an escort on the starboard bow was the USS Arkansas, and the destination became apparent when the men received booklets describing life in England.

On January 27th, Ireland was sighted, and an escort of British planes was provided along with an aircraft carrier. The George Washington dropped anchor in Liverpool, England at midnight January 28th. At 2:00 pm the next day she was tied up at her pier opposite the Capetown Castle carrying the 22nd Infantry. The men lined the rails to get their first view of England. Frank must have been struck with the small dinky engines and railroad boxcars being shuttled about the yard. Then there were the buildings mostly brick and stone with multiple chimneys. When the men spotted some young girls the rush to starboard was so great that the ship started to list dangerously to where it took the military police to shift enough men to restore the ship to an even keel. As the sun was setting, I imagine Frank was thinking just what did lie ahead of him before he could return home again.

The men began disembarking at 9:15 pm on January 29th with two companies of the 4th Engineer Combat Battalion being the first and the 3rd Battalion of the 12th being the last to leave the ship at 6:15 pm January 30th. Without delay, the troops, after marching through the streets of Liverpool, boarded the London, Midland and Scottish Railway after the American Red Cross handed out cigarettes and coffee. Indeed, this was a strange land compared to the states, but the troops heard many yell, "Welcome Yanks!" The train traveled through the beautiful countryside of rolling hills and pasture and passed through the town of Hereford and at Salisbury the men were allowed to detrain for a stretch and a cup of coffee. The train passed through the tunnel at Bristol and in the darkness of night arrived at the destination, the Devonshire City of Exeter.

Regimental Headquarters and the Medical Detachment were established at Higher Barracks in Exeter. Frank's 1st Battalion was housed a mile south of Exeter at an army post known as Bye-Pass Camp. Along with the 1st Battalion were the 4th Quartermaster Co., 4th Ordnance Co., the 36th US Station hospital and two Army postal units. The 3rd Battalion was housed at Burleigh-Salterton overlooking the English Channel. The 2nd Battalion, Cannon, and Antitank was located at Exmouth while 4th Division Headquarters was located at Tiverton, 14 miles north of Exeter. At Honiton, 18 miles east of Exeter was housed the 8th Infantry and the 22nd

Infantry was located at Newton Abbott, 30 miles to the Southwest. Due to the wide dispersal of the 4th Division, it was impossible to train except as a squad or platoon unit. (5)

On January 20th, on board the ship, George Washington, Frank sent his first letter home by V-Mail, which meant it was reviewed, that is censored by his platoon officer. V-Mail was short for Victory Mail and was used in WWII as the primary and secure method to correspond with soldiers stationed outside the United States. The soldier's letter would be censored, copied to film and printed back to paper upon arrival at its destination and reduced the cost of transferring a letter through the military postal system. Frank wrote, *"At this writing I'm on board ship somewhere on the high seas. I am feeling swell and didn't get seasick. Mac was sick for two days, but he is ok now. The food is good here and tonight we will have a show. There is much I would like to write about this trip, but that will have to wait till I get home. I will write an airmail letter and mail it the same time I send the V-mail. Let me know which gets home first. Don't worry about me. I know everything will turn out ok and that it won't be long before I will be heading back home. Love to all the family, your son, Frank."* (6)

Another letter followed dated January 31st and somehow escaped the censorship. *"Dear Mother & Dad, Somewhere in England. I am now in England. I am well and happy and while I am here, I intend to see some of the things I used to read about in geography and history books. I am quite busy, but as soon as I'm settled, I shall get caught up with my letters. Send me Vic's (Regone) and Mannie's address. They may be somewhere near my post, and I might get a chance to see them when I get a pass. It is a nice country here, and I will enjoy every minute of the time I'm here."*

February 1st was the first day Frank received a letter from home dated January 12th, that was sent first to Ft Jackson. He wrote back the same day that he had not been to town yet because his uniform has to be pressed first. He had turned in his American money in exchange for English money and already found out that English beer tasted much different from American beer. A small glass cost about 10 cents and a large cup sells for a shilling, which is about 20 cents. On February 5th, Frank wrote that he gave his uniform to an English boy to get pressed. When he brought it back, he had a nice talk with him. Frank gave him a pack of cigarettes and the boy was very pleased. Cigarettes in England cost about 50 cents a pack and all sweets and candy is rationed. When they march through a village, all the little kids run alongside and ask for gum. He said the food was good, and the barracks are the best in the area. There was a British service club just a few yards from their barracks, and they can get coffee, cake and beer there. On this same day, February 5th, the Allied Supreme Commander, General Dwight D. Eisenhower accompanied by British Air Marshal Sir Arthur Tedder, General Omar N. Bradley and Major General Raymond O. Barton, the 4th Division commander, arrived at Higher Barracks in Exeter. General Eisenhower spoke to the officers of the 12th impressing upon them the solemn responsibility, which the American people had entrusted to them. (7)

After one week, Frank started to sightsee and enjoy the beautiful English countryside. He wished he had his movie camera to take color pictures, but that was not possible. Frank was concerned that his parents would now worry since he was overseas and getting close to the war front. He wrote, *"Don't worry about me as I'm not worrying even a little bit. The only thing I would worry about is you and Dad worrying. I don't even feel conscious of being overseas. It just seems as though I'm in another state. I really like it here, and that helps a good deal."* Then he asked them to send him single edge razor blades and candy since these items were scarce in England.

The Devon countryside was beautiful, and the yellow primrose was already in bloom for the spring of 1944. The town people were very gracious and everywhere the GI's went the children would call out, *"Have some gum Chum?"* In a letter to his brother Al, he said England was just like being in the states except that traffic travels on the opposite side of the street, and the money is so different. It was payday and instead of dollars he was paid in pounds. A pound is worth about $4.00 in exchange. They had a British USO where he could get coffee and beer and a PX where cigarettes cost three pence a pack, which is about six cents in American money. Razor blades were rationed to two per week while candy and gum were also rationed. Frank signed off the letter as Cheerio, so he was indeed getting into the English culture. His letter, sent by Air Mail for 6 cents postage, was censored by William A. Forbes, 2nd Lt., Platoon Officer, which would continue until D-Day.

A baseball league was started among the 12th units and attracted the interests of quite a few British. The 4th Infantry Band and the Royal Marine Band made various tours, and the American Red Cross Clubmobiles were always a welcome sight to the troops. The chief sources of news that Frank liked to read were the weekly

Yank and the daily Stars and Stripes. The company continued its regular physical training while in England with calisthenics and marches. Frank said on February 11th that they were getting ready to fall out and start a march. Then in a letter of February 14th, Valentine's Day, he wrote, *"Since yesterday was Sunday I was able to get to town on a pass during the daytime. I visited an ancient cathedral in this town, and it was really a fine bit of architecture. It is about nine hundred years old. It's amazing that these people so long ago would erect a work that you would think could only be done by modern machinery and methods."* What Frank had visited that Sunday was the Exeter Cathedral in Exeter, England, just a few miles from their camp.

Figure 102 Exeter Cathedral

He was correct in saying the cathedral was ancient since it dated from 1107 when it was dedicated to St. Peter and St. Mary. The building went through several changes and additions through the years and took on the Gothic style, being completed in 1400. Frank saw some damage to the cathedral since on May 4, 1942, during an air raid over Exeter, there was a direct hit by a large high explosive bomb on the chapel of St James, demolishing it completely. Fortunately, several documents and artifacts were removed before the attack. Later a surprise occurred, when during repairs and clearing of the area, portions of earlier structures appeared, part of which was a Roman city and the original cathedral. (8)

Figure 103 Exeter Cathedral Today

Letters to Frank, which were delayed due to the overseas transfer, started showing up on February 16th, 14 letters in all. In fact, two were mailed from England to the States and back to England again. Letters from home were taking anywhere from 7 to 14 days to arrive. What a difference in today's mail when we transmit and receive in seconds from around the world.

Frank had some time off on February 16th and went to Exeter. When returning, the town was in a blackout, so he missed the bus stop, and before he knew it, was way off his course. Then while trying to get back his bearings he collided with a post. Next time he will know better to return when light. Frank was finding the English cuisine to be quite good. He wrote on February 19th, *"Was into town again on a pass with Mac. We had a dinner at the Salvation Army Canteen and then went to a show. They have some pretty good theaters here. There is one great difference, though. Even in the best shows you are permitted to smoke. I'm feeling tip top so don't you worry even a little bit. Just keep the letters coming this way and I won't even know that I'm away from home."*

By the end of February, Frank started receiving packages from home including cookies and candy. They arrived in excellent shape and without doubt helped boost his moral. He also received letters from his cousin Vic Regone and brother in law, Mannie Costa and they expressed a desire to meet up if they could at some rendezvous location in England. Frank and Vic Santangelo were invited to a home on Sunday night, February 27th that was outside of Exeter. He writes on Tuesday, February 29th, *"Last Sunday night Vic and I had tea at a home outside of the city. I expected to get tea and cakes but was I surprised when I saw some real fried eggs and bacon.*

Needless to say, we both had an order of eggs." At this time, the soldiers were only getting powered milk and eggs so the real thing must have tasted magnificent. Later in May Frank wrote home that he met a cute girl with a swell personality by the name of Nancy Underhill. He said he met her some time ago and had taken her out a few times. I surmise that the home they were invited to with the tea and eggs was most likely the home of Nancy Underhill.

Figure 104 Nancy Underhill and Frank

Frank was shy to write home right away about his newfound girlfriend, so it did not show up in a letter until May 10th. He enclosed a picture in this letter of Nancy and himself in front of a typical English country house with a thatch roof. Now I suspect that this was a casual girlfriend that Frank probably met at the USO, and graciously invited her out on a few dates seeing a movie or the sights in Exeter. One thing for sure though is that the pictures in his billfold were those of Virginia MacInnis of whom he had a yearlong relationship by correspondence.

On February 29th, Frank and Vic Santangelo along with other officers and noncoms were sent to a particular school some distance from Bye Pass Camp and were housed in a different camp, which Frank remarked was not nearly as good. At this location, Frank and other sergeants were receiving specialized training, which he was not allowed to divulge. I believe this training was done at the U. S. Assault Training Center at Braunton, England, which is 46 miles to the northwest of Exeter. Lt. Col. James S. Luckett, the regimental executive officer, took a detail of 25 officers and 123 enlisted men to learn how to organize assault boat teams, how to overcome hedgehogs, the procedure for debarking from landing craft and assaulting a hostile shore along with knocking out fortified positions. He did not finish this training until March 10th and returned to Bye Pass Camp. (9)

On about the last day in Braunton, he bought a walking stick with a dogs head carved on it and sent it home as a gift for Uncle Bill Ireland. Several years later the author ended up with this beautiful walking stick, which has an intricate carving of a Scottie's head on the handle. When he returned to Bye Pass Camp, he got a haircut in an English barbershop and wrote home with a laugh that the English call it a *"gentleman's hairdresser."*

On Saturday, March 3rd, Frank wrote that he was sending home some money orders since now he could save more money since he would draw a 20% increase in pay for overseas duty. Then he added, *"When you have time send me some of those chocolate covered cashews and dates that Tountas has. They sure will be appreciated."* Tountas was the Greek, who operated a soda fountain and candy store in Le Roy, NY. It shows that no matter how far away from home you are, there is nothing like a taste of hometown candy and homemade cookies. Frank's parents along with his Aunts established a regular practice of sending him packages containing cookies and candy.

Vic Regone, Frank's cousin, made a trip to Bye Pass Camp the week of March 5th when Frank was on specialized training. He left a note with a fellow in the camp that he was there and hoped they would be able to meet up soon. Unfortunately, that never happened, but when Frank was missing in action, Vic got a pass and took a ship to Normandy to search for Frank. Since the front lines were so close to Utah Beach the MP's would not allow him to move inland to contact Frank's outfit, so he had to return to England without any knowledge of Frank.

The first week of March, the regiment was put through combat problems without the cooperation of the weather, since it was cold and windy when they were on the English moors near Dartmoor. When they returned on the 10th, there was barely time to pack for another move. On March 13th, the regiment left Bye Pass and two other camps in Exeter for two weeks of ship to shore training with the US Navy. They moved by rail to Plymouth where they embarked on three APA's. Regimental Headquarters and Frank's 1st Battalion were assigned to the USS Barnett (APA5), 2nd

Battalion to the USS Dickman and the 3rd Battalion to the USS Bayfield. These ships were converted passenger ships used by the US Navy for the transport of troops in WWII.

Figure 105 USS Barnett APA 5

The three ships left Plymouth and headed westward through the English Channel and then north through the Irish Sea up to Scotland to the mouth of the Firth of Clyde. They continued up the Clyde to the location of Gourock, Scotland.

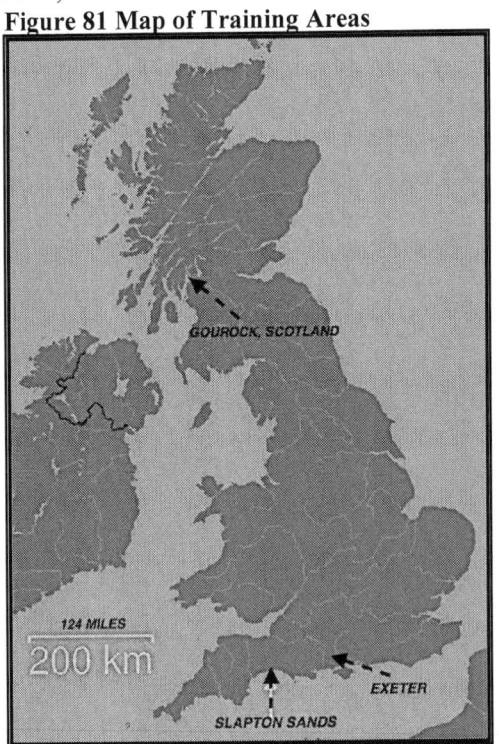

Figure 81 Map of Training Areas

At this location, there was extensive practice in organizing boat teams and reaching boat stations in a blackout. Several days were spent in learning how to debark with full equipment down rope ladders and nets. In the second week, the regiment formed into boat teams, going over the side of the ship and forming boat waves to approach a hostile shore. The men were subjected to seasickness, foul weather and cold rains throughout their training.

The military exercises were planned to achieve as much realism as possible but at the same time secure safety to prevent injuries or death. One day during the exercise, the weather started out sunny and warm while the men departed ships around 1:00 pm in the LCVPs, commonly called Higgins Boats.

Figure 107 LCVP Higgins Boat

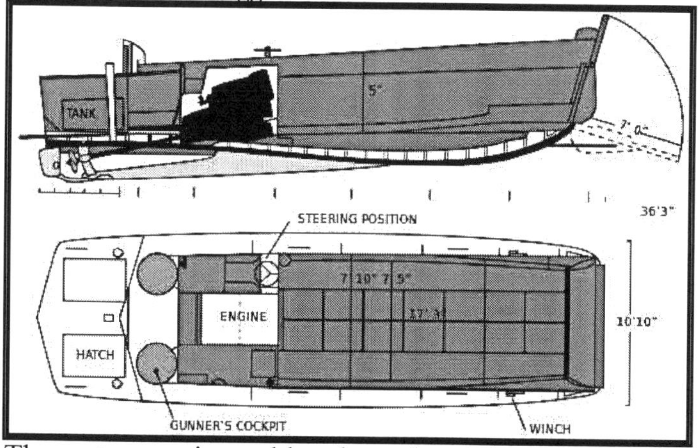

The water was icy cold and rough, so the men were subjected to seasickness and became wet to their armpits upon reaching the beach. After Frank's 1st Battalion landed the weather suddenly turned overcast with a cold rain falling. The men built driftwood fires on the beach to dry off while LCVPs returned from the USS Barnett to return the soldiers to the ship. By mid-afternoon, the wind increased in velocity, and it was taking much longer for the LCVPs to make the complete trip from the shore to the ship and harder to take on men at the shoreline. Finally, the last LCVP approached to take on the last group of men when the engine failed, and the two-man crew tried unsuccessfully to restart the engine. An LCM, a much larger vessel, then took on the men at an inlet and then tried to tow the LCVP, but the sea was too rough, and they had to abandon the effort and head back to the ship. The sea was so harsh that the men were tossed about in the LCM and several suffered injuries of broken legs and arms by the time they reached the USS Barnett. This experience demonstrated how dangerous training could be under adverse conditions. The men must have been very grateful to the Navy crew, who provided dry clothes,

Figure 108 LCM Landing Craft Mechanised

hot soup, and coffee. The exercise was at this point completed, and the ships returned to Plymouth. (10)

Packages not only arrived from home but Frank's squad received a package from the Red Cross on March 21st while they were still training off Gourock, Scotland. The men were quite surprised to find in the package, soap, razor blades, writing material, tobacco, a deck of cards and a book. Frank said it looked like Christmas for a while! On March 25th, the 12th Regiment on its return to Plymouth performed a new problem called Exercise Beaver and on March 25th, they went over the sides again and landed on a strip of beach called Slapton Sands. They did not know at the time, that they would soon return to this beach for a realistic landing under real fire. The next day all the units were back at their stations with Frank back to Bye Pass Camp in Exeter.

Then on March 26th, he received the package from home with goodies and of all things razor blades. No doubt he would be well supplied with good shaving equipment for some time. At this time, Frank was also starting to take some pictures with his camera of the English countryside. On March 27th, Frank wrote, *"I gather that Ralph Sperry hasn't changed his feelings towards the infantry. HA! Yet I so know this to be true that anyone who served in this branch of service can come back knowing that he did his share."* No finer words could be spoken!

In early April, there was a change of command for the 12th Infantry. Col. Henderson due to ill health was forced to relinquish command. General Omar Bradley requested Col. Russell P. Reeder and on April 4th, he assumed command of the 12th. He was an outstanding leader and within a short space of time, he met every officer and enlisted man in the regiment. I'm sure Frank was very impressed with him. He instilled in the men a determination to overcome whatever obstacles might lie ahead. Then he made training corrections and demonstrated his knowledge of the job to be done. Shortly after, another outstanding leader, Brigadier General Theodore Roosevelt, known as Young Teddy, became assistant division commander of the 4th Division.

The first two weeks of April included training with small units, demonstrations, and firing of German weapons, laying and detecting minefields, combat firing exercises at East Merrivale and Scorriton, antiaircraft firing with caliber .50 machine guns at Bideford and continual physical training. The third week of April, company and platoon problems were conducted at Harpford Common and Huxham Brake. (10)

When April 1st came, it wasn't without the typical April Fools joke. Sgt. Search told Frank that the first sergeant was looking for him. Frank thinking he was going to be pay guard, reported to the first sergeant who said that he did not want him for anything. Why was he there? Now it was time to pay Sgt. Search back, today if possible. The first part of April, Frank started to experience for the first time some of the English cultures. Vic and Frank went to see a ballet, and they both agreed that they wasted their time. He writes, *"It's a story told in dance form but I wasn't interested in fairy tales. We should have seen a movie instead. Don't send me any cigarettes as we can buy seven packs a week in our PX and they only cost five cents a pack."* Interesting that they were giving him cigarettes since he indicated in a previous mail that he did not smoke. Can you imagine being allowed to buy seven packs a week?

As it became close to Easter Sunday, April 9th, Frank wanted to attend Good Friday services in the nearby town, which was Exeter. Vic, Mac, and Frank put their names into the first sergeant, and they were able to attend. There was a procession in town led by a band playing hymns and a group of English marines. Then in an open enclosure, in what looked to be an auditorium, services, and Stations of the Cross were held. It turned out to be a beautiful day, and they were happy that they were able to attend. The Monday after Easter, Frank received another box of dates and chocolates and wrote back right away to say how good they were. He also asked for another box of chocolate covered cashews, so we now know that was his favorite candy.

On April 12th, apparently Frank was very optimistic concerning the ending of the war. He wrote, *"I'm still feeling fine and still enjoying my stay here in England. It looks to me as though it won't be long before this business will be over and I'll be coming back."* One wonders how you could be an optimist with all the bad news and the state of the war in early 1944. I think that Frank was now close to the end of 33 months of infantry ranger training and in seeing the full capability of his regiment he believed the enemy would see the end and surrender soon. He did not comprehend the insanity of Hitler (Germany) and ToJo (Japan).

Frank being the photographer he was, continued to take pictures in England. He wrote his sister Mary on April 13th that he needed size 620 film since Sgt. Blackman would lend Frank his camera. Frank said his camera case was damaged and was being held together with adhesive tape. Frank's letters continued to convey an attitude of optimism. On April 14th he wrote, *"I'm still feeling tip top, and I'm in high spirits. I don't worry because I don't have the time to, and secondly I like it here. The only drawback is that I can't get home on a pass like Ft Dix. But don't you worry for we all will be coming home soon."*

The love of candy did not diminish with Frank. He received a package of chocolates on April 18th and the next day he wrote home to send him a box of candy bars since they are rationed to three candy bars per week. On April 23rd he wrote, *"I'm awaiting the box of candy with an increasing appetite. Candy is really hard to get here."*

The camp entertainment was usually a movie, and since it was in camp, it would be free. On April 22nd, Frank and Mac went to a movie titled, In Old Oklahoma. It was very seldom that they could enjoy a movie in camp since there was usually a group of men that felt they could make all the noise they please. There was then a break in writing of eight days, which is unusual for Frank since he was writing a letter home every day or every other day. Why was there a span of eight days? What Frank could not write about was that they were preparing for Exercise Tiger, a comprehensive rehearsal of the Normandy invasion. Upon returning from Exercise Tiger, Frank writes on May 1st, *"Recently I have been very busy, and the situation was such that I was not able to write. If in the future there is a break in my letters don't be alarmed. It's not because I'm sick but because writing is impossible. Yesterday I received my mail all at once twelve letters, and I was awfully surprised to learn about Mannie Carli's misfortune."*

Mannie Carli was a cousin of Franks, who ran the Broadway bar and restaurant in Lime Rock. The business had been quite successful and before the war was popular as a roller skating rink and dance hall. In late April, when Mannie Carli was leaving the restaurant on the way to his car, a robber held him up. In the parking lot, Mannie was carrying a briefcase of money, and when the robber demanded he hand it over, he threw the briefcase over his shoulder. The robber at this point shot Mannie with a shotgun in the liver. The robber ran without the money, and Mannie made it to his mother's house (Aunt Lena), burst through the front door and collapsed on the living room floor. He was very fortunate to survive the shooting and lived to run the Broadway for several years. Even on the home front, you could be subjected to life-threatening danger outside of wartime service.

Frank made it a practice never to write anything that would worry his family back home and now in England all soldiers were under strict rules to never describe anything about their location, plans or training. Their letters were of course under censorship and they, in turn, were subject to severe penalties if they revealed any information that would aid the enemy. No wonder his letters contained only information on their free time such as when they saw movies, went to dances, or visited sights. The common phrase in almost all letters would be *"I'm feeling fine"*, *"like it here"*, and *"enjoying my stay here in England"*.

What the folks back home did not know was that from April 22-30, 1944, the 12th Regiment along with the 4th Division was involved in Exercise Tiger, a large-scale rehearsal for the D-Day invasion of Normandy. Exercise Tiger took place at Slapton Sands in Devon, England. On April 22nd, the regiment left Exeter for Plymouth to a marshaling area where from the 22nd to the 25th, the exercise focused on marshaling and embarkation drill. On the evening of the 26th, the first wave of men boarded the transport ships in the Plymouth Harbor. When they reached Slapton Sands on the morning of April 27th, they left their LST's and headed for shore in landing craft (Higgins Boats) just as they would in the Normandy invasion. Slapton Sands closely resembled the features of Utah Beach, where in just over a month the invasion of Normandy, France would take place. Much detail was needed to simulate the scene and conditions of landing on a fortified enemy shore. The plan was to have the first wave land at 7:30 am and was to be preceded with a live firing exercise to condition the troops to the sight, sound and smell of a naval bombardment. Live rounds were to be fired over the heads of the landing troops by ships at sea, by an

Figure 109 Map of Exercise Tiger Slapton Sands

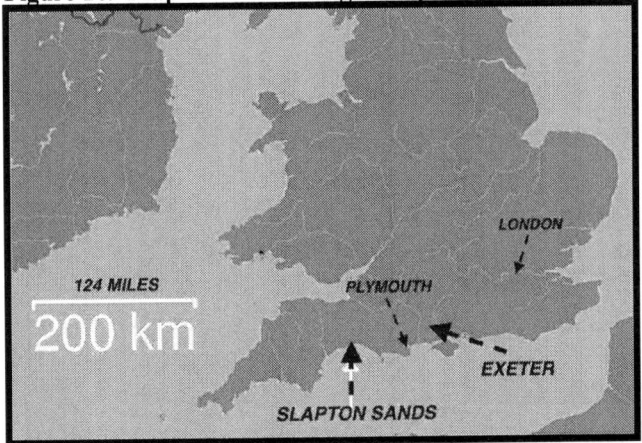

order from General Dwight D. Eisenhower, who believed the men should be conditioned by exposure to real battle conditions. The British heavy cruiser HMS Hawkins was to shell the beach with live ammunition from 6:30 to 7:00 am and then give enough time to inspect the beach and declare it safe.

However several of the landing ships that morning were behind schedule and Admiral Don P. Moon decided to delay H-hour for one hour, to 8:30 am. The HMS Hawkins received this message but not by several of the landing craft. There was a mix-up in the assignment of radio frequencies, which resulted in some getting the message of the delay and some not. The result was that troops were landing on the beach at the same time as the bombardment and this led to many men being killed or injured by friendly fire. There is no available count of casualties, since this incident of friendly fire along with another incident far worse that this, was not released for public knowledge until 40 years later.

Apparently Frank's 1st Battalion, as part of the 12th Regiment, had landed after this unfortunate incident, stormed the beach well, moved across the flooded area and seized the high ground behind the beach. After two days, April 28th and 29th, the 12th pushed back the enemy, the 29th Infantry Division, and secured all of its objectives. On April 29th after the regiment had bivouacked before moving back to Exeter, the men saw their first aerial bombing of Plymouth by the German Luftwaffe. They could hear the anti-aircraft batteries around Plymouth and witnessed an enemy plane plunging to earth on fire. The plane crashed and exploded very close to the 4th Division command post. A crewmember had bailed out of the plane and was captured by a 4th Division MP who took him prisoner. (11)

144

However what followed the 12th landing and advance on April 27th was a very grave incident now termed the Battle of Lyme Bay. The next day, April 28th, early in the morning about 2:00 am, the same LST convoy, carrying remaining troops of the 4th Division, was attacked by nine German E-boats under the command of Captain Bernd Klug in Lyme Bay. The LST convoy left Plymouth on the same transports to perform another mock landing at Slapton Sands. The convoy was simulating a circular route near the landing area as would be carried out in the Normandy invasion to achieve the correct position for a planned advance to the beachhead. Unknown to the Allies was a plan by the Germans to send E-boats out of Cherbourg, France to cross the English Channel, and torpedo ships in the Slapton Sands training exercise. A second objective was to rescue Allied soldiers for interrogation concerning an Allied invasion. The Germans needed to know what invasion tactics were planned and would they be similar to the Allied landings at Anzio and Salerno, Italy.

Two ships were assigned to protect the convoy of ships in Exercise Tiger, but only one was present, the HMS Azalea, a Corvette. A second ship, the HMS Scimitar, a WWI destroyer, had just been in a collision with an Allied LST and had structural damage so left the convoy to return to Plymouth for repairs. Since the LST's and British naval headquarters were operating on different radio frequencies, the LST's did not know their protection was diminished. Then when E-boats were sighted earlier in the night by other British ships in the Channel, the Corvette was informed, but its commander did not communicate to the LST convoy thinking that they had already been told. Also, British shore batteries at Salcombe had seen the E-boats but were ordered to hold fire because the British did not want the Germans to know that Salcombe was defended.

The HMS Azalea Corvette was leading convoy T-4, composed of eight LSTs carrying vehicles and combat engineers of the 1st Engineer Special Brigade. The E-boats launched a torpedo attack in the darkness against the convoy with devastating results. LST-507 immediately caught fire and was abandoned with the loss of 121 Army and 69 Navy personnel. LST-531 was torpedoed and sank within six minutes with a loss of 303 Army and 108 Navy personnel. LST 289 was set on fire but was able to make it to shore by a tow from LCVPs with the loss of 13 Navy personnel.

Figure 110 USS LST 289 Returning to Plymouth

Figure 111 USS LST 289 Damage to Stern

Friendly fire, unfortunately, damaged LST 511, with no casualties. Remaining ships in the convoy fought off the E-boats, and they left the fight. There were a total of 946 servicemen killed including 749 US Army personnel with about 200 wounded. Many soldiers unused to the sea put their lifebelts on incorrectly, so when they entered the water, the weight of their combat packs flipped them onto their backs, dragging their heads underwater and drowning them.

Their superiors swore all survivors to secrecy over concerns of information leaks so close to the planned Normandy invasion. However, there was a serious problem since there were ten missing officers with top-level clearance for D-Day. Since they knew the invasion plans, they could be compromised if they were captured and interrogated. A meticulous search was conducted for bodies of the serviceman and as a result, all ten missing officers were accounted for as dead. Due to the circumstances, there was a hasty treatment of the bodies with a mass burial in the Devon countryside. The location of this burial site is to this day unknown. Victim's families were not notified until August 1944 to guard against divulging information about the upcoming Normandy invasion. When they were informed it was stated, they were killed on D-Day, June 6th. Some of this information was released in the Stars and Stripes military newspaper by midsummer 1944, but due to the war activity, it caught little notice.

It was not publicized in detail to the general public until many years after the war in a book written by Ken Small in 1988 titled, The Forgotten Dead. There were several lessons learned from the mistakes made in Exercise Tiger, which included standardized radio frequencies for the Allied forces, improved life vest training for troops and a plan for boats to pick up floating survivors on D-Day. (12)

Frank was very fortunate, as was the entire 12th Regiment, of any harm from these practice landings at Slapton Sands. They arrived late enough on April 27th to not encounter the friendly fire in the first wave of landing and early enough not be caught in the early morning, 2:00 am, April 28th attack by German E-boats. That was indeed fortunate but time would soon come when the regiment would suffer significant casualties from D-Day all the way to war end.

Early in May the regiment test fired all of their weapons and did trial loadings of vehicles. Vehicles and radio equipment that had not been previously waterproofed were finished. On one evening General Bradley addressed all the officers of the 4th Division at Exeter and left them saying, *"See you all soon on the beaches."* Frank would not have been present, but I'm sure heard of the event.

Frank was now close to finishing his time in England. On May 5th, he wrote that he received all at once three letters from home, 25th, 27th, and 28th. He also received a letter from his little brother Billy, who had just started to write to his big brother. Frank mentions that he will increase his allotment for his home savings account by $25 on June 1st, since he says, *"Its one way of saving and a good way to keep from spending it foolishly."* At this time, Frank lost his wristwatch when the strap broke and could not find it after searching the area where he was last. It appears that Frank did not have a watch on D-Day since they were not issued watches as Government Issue.

May 8th, Frank, and Bob Leonard went to Mr. Hookways and had a good dinner. Joe Louis, the prizefighter, put on a boxing exhibition, but Frank choose not to go. Frank states, *"I'm feeling fine and trust that everyone at home is well. Wish I could go fishing with Al. Bob wants to get some tackle and go fishing here. We will have to look up the English hunting and fishing laws first, though."* To pass the time and to subdue the fear of what lie ahead, talking about your favorite sport or hobby would only be natural.

On May 10th, Frank witnessed a beautiful spring in Devon, England. The weather turned warm; the lilacs were in bloom, and the English flower gardens were exploding in color. Frank wished he had his movie camera so he could record the colors. Then in his May 11th letter he wrote, *" Vic and I plan to celebrate our three years the night of the fifteenth. It certainly has been a long year, but my hopes are high."* Three years of concentrated military training would soon be put into action.

Then on May 12th, Frank knew that they would soon be departing for marshaling yards in Plymouth. In his letter home, *"From your letter I gather that you hadn't received any mail from me for a week. At one time I was kept pretty busy and couldn't write. There will be times when there will be a lapse in my letters so don't worry for I shall always write when I have the chance. I'm always feeling tip top. Went to town on pass recently with Bob (Leonard) and Vic and had a darn good time. We always have a lot of fun when we go out."* Frank was preparing them for a time lapse between letters, and that would indeed place a burden of fear on the family.

Bob and Frank went to Exeter and saw a Russian ballet with some folk dances on May 13th and thought it was a good show, a departure from the first ballet he saw a few months ago. The men tried to enjoy the simple things in life even a crow. Frank writes on May 14th, *"Recently one of the fellows caught a wild crow and brought it back to the barracks. It's a young bird and rather tame so today I snapped a picture of the crow perched on top of a bald headed soldier. It ought to be pretty good if it turns out ok."* The author has not found the picture and believes it was still in the camera, which was probably lost at this crucial time.

May 16th the regiment left Exeter for the Plymouth marshaling yard. They were temporarily stationed at Plummer and Seaton Barracks. The 12th was at this time sealed in, so there was no further communication with the outside world except through receiving letters and sending out censored letters.

At the new barracks in Plymouth, Frank wrote a letter to his sister Mary, May 17th. He tells her that he has received her letters, but is unable to answer all the letters since he doesn't always have the time. He writes, *"When I do have time off from duty I don't want to spend all of it writing letters."* He had sent a portrait of himself taken back in Camp Gordon and asked to have it colored. Mary had sent it to his friend Bob, and he thought the coloring was quite good. His last line in the letter was, *"Let's hear how you jitterbugs are getting along, Signing off, Frank"*. This letter was the last Frank would send to his sister.

In a letter home on May 17th, Frank asks for the date of Ray Regone's wedding and would like his sister Mary to take some movies of it for him. He sure would like his movie camera but admits it is impossible to get movie film in England. Apparently Mom could only send three candy bars at one time, so he told her not to bother. They did send a large box of candy because I remember as a child it was returned one or two months later, box crushed and the candy waterlogged and spoiled. It most likely went to England and then returned due to the timing of the Normandy invasion.

On May 18th, Vic and Frank went to a free show in camp and saw Honeymoon Lodge. He wrote, *"I enjoyed it for the laughs that were in it. For our noon meal today we had roast beef. It was exceptionally good which speaks well for the cooks as I am pretty critical where food is concerned. I haven't had a good dish of spaghetti for a long time, though. Guess I'll have to wait till I come home."*

May 20th, Sgt. Search, Sgt. Kotrla and Frank got a pass and visited a nearby town where they met two English sailors in a pub and had quite a chat. One sailor had been to New York City and was quite impressed. Frank had not received the package of candy yet and was anxiously awaiting its arrival. The next day a letter from home indicated that they had quite a bit of company from Buffalo and Billy was disappointed in losing his teacher, Mrs. Strobel and getting a new one for the next school term.

The final briefings were now starting to take place in Plymouth. The master plan was that CT-12 would land according to landing diagram on Beaches Green and Red (Utah Beach) and then advance inland initially with two battalions abreast to seize objectives shown on a briefing map. The master plan was called Top Secret Field Order No. 1 issued May 20, 1944. Each soldier now received this information through his squad leader on what the objective was, and how it was to be carried out. The order was illustrated on a large wall map and with aerial photographs. The 4th Infantry was to be supported by air and naval task forces and would invade the Cotentin Peninsula of France on D-Day to capture Cherbourg. The Naval Task Force would provide transport, protection at sea, gunfire support and destroy all underwater obstacles. Air support would be provided by the IX Tactical Air Command, and the 101st Airborne would land by glider and parachute in areas west of Turqueville with the mission of assisting the landing of the 4th Division. The 82nd Airborne Division would land by glider and parachute near the Merderet River. It would capture Ste. Mere Elise and south to Beauzeville Au Plain to reach the 101st Airborne. The 4th Division orders were to locate and assist the 101st and 82nd Airborne Divisions and to relieve them.

Aerial photographs were issued down to every squad leader, and each platoon leader would assemble his men around a large rubber replica of the Cotentin Peninsula, complete in every minute detail of roads, bridges, buildings, hedgerows, fortifications, and obstacles. The platoons and squads studied the model calculating the best routes of approach and taking advantage of every terrain feature. The only question now remaining was when would D-Day occur?

The 12th was also briefed, that on the other side of the channel on the Cotentin Peninsula, was the German 709th Infantry Division with the 243rd Infantry Division in reserve. They knew the strength and composition of these divisions and that the enemy could bring up another infantry division and two panzer divisions very quickly. South of the landing area the Germans had already brought in another division and a company of tanks. On the west of Utah Beach, there was the possibility of six 380 mm guns operated by 300 men. All signs were that the Germans were expecting a frontal attack on Cherbourg since they knew the Allies desperately needed a seaport to bring in a massive amount to supplies. Yes, they were indeed wrong on the landing location and instead would receive an attack on Cherbourg from the south. (11)

While in the Plymouth camp waiting for the order to embark for the invasion, the men went to movies in camp or would play baseball if weather permitted. The work was primarily finished now, so there was time to kill.

The result of the German Blitz in 1941 and 1942 left the city of Plymouth in ruins, and it is a wonder that there were facilities available for soldiers to enjoy. The bomb damage was near the center of the city with outlying districts not so severely damaged.

So most of the soldiers would enjoy the camp, USO, and Red Cross facilities.

Figure 112 Plymouth After Blitz

Frank watched a baseball game on Tuesday, May 22nd between their company and another. Vic was the umpire and apparently did a fair job since no one wanted to kill him afterward. On May 24th, the men were still waiting for orders with not much to do. Frank in the afternoon went out on a short hike. When he returned, he met the mail orderly bringing in the mail and with it the package from home with candy. He writes, *"That candy was surely welcome. Vic also was delighted, as he likes Tountas Chocolates as well as I. His girl sends him Fanny Farmers so between you and his girl we always have a treat when a package arrives. Last night I got a pass and went for a walk. Later in the evening I went to a fish and chip restaurant but instead of the usual fish and chips they served sausage and chips. The sausage was about ten percent meat and ninety percent cornmeal. It wasn't very tasty."*

On May 25th, Frank went to a concert given by the official US Army band. He says, *"Boy that's some band. Before I was in the service, I had often heard the band broadcast. It used to be on the Army Hour and led by Captain Darcy. He led the band last night, and I believe anyone who went to the concert didn't regret it. Don't bother to get me a watch, as I probably would lose it or break it. I always did have bad luck with watches. I'm feeling fine and full of pep. Hope all are well at home."*

May 27th, *"I had almost forgotten that this was my birthday. Remembered it when I went to mass this afternoon. I couldn't get my usual quart of ice cream this year but this morning I had a real honest to goodness orange. And that in itself was a treat as they are*

151

pretty hard to find over here. The boys had a ball game started when we got back, so I played ball for a while. It was the first time I've played in years."

May 28th, *"It has been a swell sunny Sunday afternoon here. This morning I went to mass and communion. In the afternoon, I wrote a letter but didn't do much of anything else. Tonight for supper we had a pretty good plate, meat, mashed potatoes, carrots, peas, pineapple and two delicious oranges."*

May 30th, *"I have some enlarged pictures of the snaps I sent you before, so I will send them along in the next letter. They are not much better as they are quite dark. Although you can't see it, I still have my mustache. It has been the best of many a joke, but I'm stubborn and refuse to shave it off. One day when I was in the dispensary getting some nose drops, the Colonel was there. He watched the medic for a minute, then he says, sergeant what's he doing cultivating that bush. I think my face turned a little red from that one. HA."*

This is the last letter Frank would write home so I will state it completely:

Sgt. F. W. Brown
32131532 Co C 1Bn
12th Inf. APO4 c/o Pm NY, NY
May 31, 44
Dear Mother & Dad,

Haven't much to write tonight. At the present time, I'm having a lot of fun watching Sgt. Blackman swatting a few flies that share our room. Sgt. Search, Vic and I are shouting encouragement as Sam darn near knocks the building down with his improvised flyswatter.

We went to a show here tonight. I had seen the picture once before, but I stayed and saw it once more.

I'm feeling fine and hope everyone at home are ok. Have been having it easy for a few days, so I'm feeling super fine.

Must sign off now. Love to all the family,
Your son,
Frank

On June 1-3,1944, 13 LCI's, 6 LCT's and 5 LST's were loaded with all the 12th Infantry's 3000 soldiers, vehicles, and equipment. The 12th Regiment left Plymouth Harbor with a clear sky on June 4th, barrage balloons hovering overhead and moved into the English Channel.

Figure 113 Plymouth Marshaling Yards

They then moved into tiny inlets and waited for the order to group for the channel crossing. The next day was bright and sunny but what followed were clouds and a steady wind, which caused choppiness in the channel. By mid-afternoon, the LCI's moved out of their holding places and entered the rough waters of the channel. The largest invasion armada in history, 5000 vessels, and 160000 troops, moved east in the approaching darkness and were flanked with a protection of cruisers and destroyers.

The invasion of Normandy had begun! (12)

Psalm 146:5-6 "Blessed is he whose help is the God of Jacob, whose hope is in the Lord his god, the Maker of heaven and earth, the sea, and everything in them----the Lord, who remains faithful forever."

"****"

Chapter Fourteen

Normandy D-Day
June 4 to 8 1944

Note: The book, History of the Twelfth Infantry Regiment in WWII, by Gerden F. Johnson, was a valuable resource in writing this chapter since it provided detailed information on the Utah Beach landing leading to the battle in which Frank sacrificed his life for our freedom.

On June 4, 1944, the 12th Infantry left Plymouth Harbor on thirteen LCIs, six LCTs, and five LSTs. Frank with his platoon was on board an LCI, Landing Craft Infantry, which would hold around 200 men. (10)

Figure 114 Landing Craft Infantry LCI

There was a barrage balloon floating above each vessel, which would defend against enemy dive-bombers. Barrage balloons would have tethered cables that could release and hang onto a wing and thereby bring the aircraft down.

The convoy moved into the English Channel and then into small inlets to wait. The officers and noncoms made last minute studies of maps and checked over their equipment. The next day, June 5th, was sunny and warm. Clouds soon gathered overhead, and the wind increased to cause the channel to be very choppy. The word was then given that the next day, June 6th was D-Day, with H-hour at 6:30 am! The middle of the afternoon on June 5th, the vessels left the inlets and through rough waves turned east in the Channel. They moved across the channel in alignment protected by cruisers and destroyers. Into the darkness of night, they moved, east toward the Normandy shore of France.

June 6th broke with a cold, icy rain accompanied by rolling clouds and blustery winds, which had blown for several hours. There was a good chop on the sea and along the coast of Normandy; the surf was heavy on the beaches. On the vessels, the 12th was awakened out of cramped sleeping quarters and men climbed to the upper decks. There before them was a sight that must have met Frank with almost unbelief. If you could see through the mist and rain, there were 4000 ships, the largest armada of naval vessels in history, including army, navy, combat vessels, cargo vessels, and large landing craft. In view were battleships and cruisers, destroyers, gunboats, corvettes and destroyer escorts, frigates and rocket ships, minesweepers, transports, landing craft of all sizes, service ships, hospital ships, tug boats, dispatch boats, and Coast Guard rescue cutters. In all of this were seasick infantrymen, not in a mood to play cards or craps but very somber in the thought of what lie ahead. Since Frank liked to send letters every other day, I'm sure it crossed his mind that he should be writing a letter about now. He was aware that the family back home would soon worry upon hearing the news and not getting the reassurance of a letter. No time for that now, just time to prepare for the inevitable.

For hours, there was the sound of airplanes moving southward and returning. Eyes strained skyward for the dreaded Luftwaffe and seaward for German submarines and E-boats. By the grace of God, the enemy did not appear. Frank on the LCI experienced a din of silence; written in every man's face the fearful anticipation of what was to come. Then nine miles offshore, the battleships placed themselves in a position to come broadside of the shore ready to fire salvos at the coastal guns and fortifications, to support soon advancing infantry. Then closer to shore were the cruisers, destroyers and patrol boats and closer yet trawlers were sweeping the surface for mines. The first wave into Utah Beach was the 4th Division, 8th, and 22nd Regiments.

Now all the planning on paper and practiced in exercises was taking place before their very eyes. Most of these men had experienced three years of about 800 various exercises consisting of 250 marches, 400 tactical problems, and around 40 specialized schools. They were the most skilled and trained warrior force in American military history. Although only a minority had seen actual combat, they were highly trained and ready with high morale. Indeed, they were fighting brothers!

A few of the men in his squad must have been seasick, but it was doubtful if Frank was since previously he was not susceptible to seasickness. The Navy skippers of the LCI's had a large map in front of them and knew when to discharge their men. This moment had been practiced at Slapton Sands beach where the conditions were made real except now they had harsh weather. However as the morning wore on the 12th got a break in the weather when the sun broke through the clouds, and the waters calmed.

When the Normandy coast became visible, there were columns of black smoke on the left of Utah Beach. The 8th Infantry had landed at H-hour, 6:30 am and had destroyed fortifications, while the 22nd Infantry, on the right, was still in a battle near burning pillboxes. A mile behind the beach you could just make out the steeple of a church in St. Martin de Varreville. Frank would have been in an LCI (Landing Craft Infantry), which could carry around 200 troops and then would have transferred over to an LCVP (Landing Craft Vehicle Personnel), commonly called a Higgins Boat. The Higgins Boat, operated by the U. S. Coast Guard, would have held his squad plus one other. After the LCI had discharged their troops to the Higgins Boats, they made their run for the shore. Frank may have noticed that something was wrong, as the terrain did not appear as studied in the maps and rubber model back in England. The sides of a Higgins Boat were high enough that it was hard to see over them but low enough that icy cold salt water would splash the men in their face. Commands were given to check rifles, which were loaded and ready. Frank's equipment at the time was a typical combat GI, which included a pack, shovel, bandoliers of ammunition, two grenades, a life belt, first aid, maps, compass, and of course his M-1 rifle.

I believe the primary thought in Frank's mind when the Higgins Boat struck bottom was to push quickly through the water, reach the sandy beach, and quickly gain cover. The approach must have seemed like an eternity especially when seeing bursts of shells hit the beach from German artillery. After he and his squad had reached the seawall, the order was to push off immediately inland.

It was 10:30 am when Col. "Red" Reeder and Lt. Col. Dominick Montalbano and the 2nd Battalion landed on the beach two miles south of Red Beach where they were supposed to land. The incorrect location caused a period of disorganization of the companies. On the right the 1st Battalion commanded by Lt. Col. Charles Jackson headed ashore. The beach was feeling the impact of German guns a few miles from shore. Frank would have heard the roar of artillery, mortars exploding and the occasional machine gun fire. The beach at this point was littered with burning craft and equipment including trucks, jeeps, dukws, strewn throughout the beach damaged and burning. Many landing craft, which did not make it was littered on the shore. Then there was the sight of dead and wounded Americans lying in the shell holes. What Frank was seeing was the results of the first wave of the 4th Division that landed in the past four hours. The adrenalin must have been driving every soldier along with Frank to get off the beach as fast as possible and gain cover. All the training over the past three years was now in play for every soldier. Scared, darn right, but driven to accomplish the mission.

There were holes blown in the seawall by the engineers and lines of white tape had been laid where it was safe from being blown

Figure 115 Map of 12th Infantry Advance

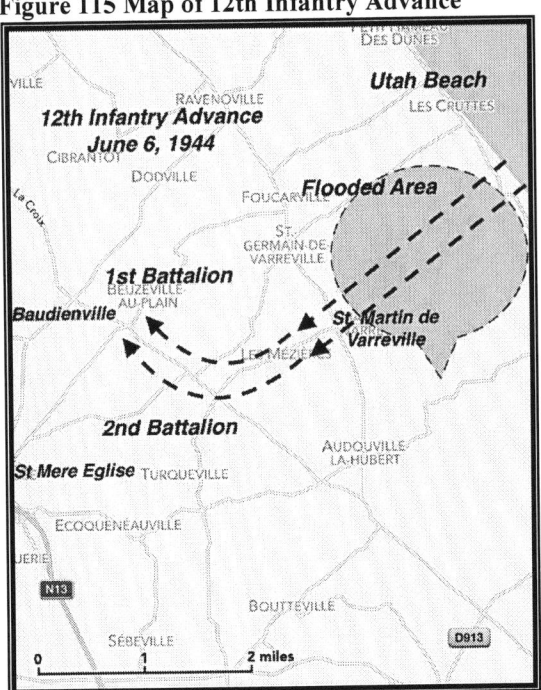

up by mines. After moving off the beach, the first obstacle was to go through the waist deep 1500 yards of flooded area, which the Germans caused as a deterrent to advancing troops. Trenches crisscrossed the flooded area so that a soldier weighted down with equipment would suddenly disappear beneath the surface and thankfully come up due to his Mae West life belt. The water was cold and murky and soaked the soldiers through. Frank's photos in his wallet, which was returned to his parents later, showed the effect of water and mold. At this time, the few roads or causeways were jammed by slowly moving equipment and now and then would appear an ominous sign, "Achtung! Minen!" intended to cause pause to any soldier. However, the sappers had already moved ahead clearing and marking the way free of mines.

Frank may not have known that the regimental command landed at 11:40 am and was preparing to set up a command post, CP, not far behind. The other side of the flooded area at the village of St. Martin de Varreville, the units would have assembled each into its correct position for Battalion 1 and 2. Frank would have witnessed Col. Red Reeder directing the assembly of each battalion in proper battle formation. Now the landing took place two miles from their planned sectors, so the success of the regiment depended on the skillful judgment of the commanders. There was confusion as the battalion companies sought their planned battle position but under the leadership of officers and noncoms this quickly evolved. Frank in the 1st Battalion was the first to assemble under the command of Lt. Col. Jackson and to move toward the objective Cherbourg. The plan of the attack was to have two battalions abreast, around 2000 men. The 1st Battalion was on the right and the 2nd Battalion on the left and the plan was to move westward toward a road junction a half mile from St. Martin de Varreville, then turn 45 degrees and move northward toward Montebourg. The 3rd Battalion was to follow the 1st Battalion and to contact the 502nd Parachute Regiment and 746th Tank Battalion at St. Mere Elise.

The battalions started moving forward at 1:30 pm, just three hours after their landing. Enemy fire was soon encountered coming from the hedgerows, trees, and sunken roads, which were prevalent in this area. Now and then men from the 82 Airborne would appear, some wounded and telling of their terrible landings by parachute or in smashed up gliders. The enemy showed no mercy when paratroopers descended and were shot in the air or upon hitting the ground. During this slow advancement, 90 yards and then 200 yards, Col Red Reeder inspired the men by suddenly appearing and urging the men onward. I imagine Frank must have been struck with the courage of this officer who inspired them to advance into enemy fire. Col. Red Reeder was severely wounded a few days later and received the Distinguished Service Cross for his gallantry. Frank as part of the 1st Battalion reached an enemy position west of Beauzeville Au Plain, which they completely demolished. At this time many German soldiers battered by our forces were surrendering, sometimes two or three and in small groups. As evening soon approached, Frank witnessed the second landings of gliders with our troops, which came in from the sea. Many of them crashed on landing, and one fell close to the 1st Battalion First Aid Station, where men rushed forward to give aid to those inside the glider. The 1st and 2nd Battalion fought the Germans hard during the landings to prevent the enemy from firing at the gliders. The regiment did not stop fighting until dark, and Frank along with his weary squad dug slit trenches and broke open their K rations.

The night of June 6th was indeed a long sleepless night. Frank must have been extremely tired that night with a full moon in a cloudless sky revealing the landscape around them. There was a stream of gliders in the darkness that continued for some time during the night with about half of them cracking up with death and casualties. The regiment fought even harder to prevent the Germans from firing on the gliders. Intermittent rifle and machine gun fire would occur, and then artillery shells would roar in the distance and the resultant earth pounding explosions. All night long the Germans tried the perimeter defenses of the 1st Battalion only to die by a bullet or a hand grenade. Then Germans threw smoke grenades into the battalion trying to create panic by simulating a gas attack, but the troops were prepared. At this time, the 3rd Battalion moved into position to the rear of the 1st Battalion to be ready at dawn to protect the rear from attack. The 8th Infantry was now on the left flank and the 22nd Infantry on the right to resume the attack north to Cherbourg. The end of the first day, June 6th, the 4th Division although behind schedule had already accomplished much.

On June 7th in the early morning hours, the 1st and 2nd Battalions tried to get some sleep. During the night patrols from Company B found a German 88 mm gun and destroyed it. At 6:00 am Frank's squad would have had breakfast of cold K and D rations and would have checked their weapons and secured grenades and ammunition as necessary. In the first hour, Frank in Company C experienced machine gun fire only a quarter mile away. The slope of the terrain gently sloped upward giving the enemy an advantage. Then at 10:00 am, south of Bandienville the 1st Battalion met resistance from several homes where the Germans had heavy machine guns. The 2nd Battalion on the left flank was fighting in the village of Neuville Au Plain.

Figure 116 Map of 12th Infantry on June 8, 1944

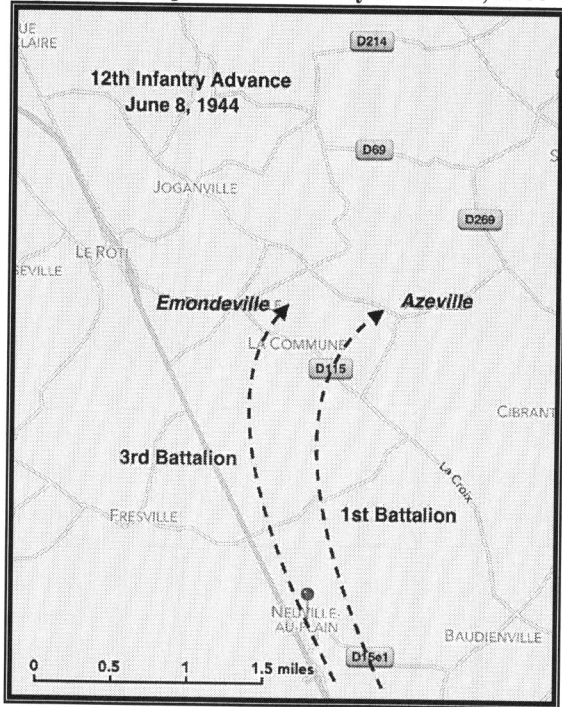

In house to house fighting the Germans had machine pistols, machine guns, and rifles shooting from the windows protected by thick walls of masonry. Frank would have heard American and British planes overhead speedily heading north to hit the German supply routes and their forces heading south. At 10:15 am the 1st Battalion, using mortar fire blew the enemy held houses and slowly surged forward. They were halted south of the main road to Azeville and found shelter along the many hedgerows along the road. Col. Reeder saw a gap between the two battalions and moved the 3rd Battalion abreast of the 1st and put the 2nd into reserve.

At 2:30 pm the lines were consolidated and the men dug in while Naval gunfire hit the Germans in the town of Emondeville. Major Gerden F. Johnson, the executive officer of the 1st Battalion, moved the 12th Regiment CP forward but found themselves so close to Emondeville that they came under heavy enemy fire. Quick action required them to retreat and set up the CP at Saussetour. At 11:30 am the German mortars were now finding their range and causing many American casualties. At the same time, many German prisoners were coming into the 1st and 3rd Battalions. At this time the 12th was able to identify the enemy as an anti-tank battalion of the German 7th Army, the 2nd Company of the 705th Georgian Regiment, one ambulance section of the 709th Medical

161

Battalion and the 1st and 13th Companies of the 919th Infantry Regiment. The 12th seeing its first combat of the war was confronting an experienced war fighting machine from the North African and Eastern Front.

At 5:15 pm the 2nd Battalion, which was being held in reserve in the rear of the 1st and 3rd Battalion, reported it was engaged in a fight with the enemy, which was attempting to circle the 12th on the left and right flank. When word was received the CP was pulled to the center and the battalions were grouped more tightly together. If the Germans had succeeded in cutting the 12th off to the rear, the enemy would have had a straight shot to the beachhead and caused considerable havoc.

On June 8th, the ground situation around the 12th remained unchanged. The 1st Battalion was on the right, the 3rd on the left and the 2nd in the rear as a reserve. At 5:30 am, Naval gunfire pounded the town of Emondeville for about one hour. Frank would have heard each 16-inch shell hit the town, and the sound must have been deafening just a half-mile away. The 1st and 3rd Battalions moved slowly forward and received many casualties from heavy German artillery fire. At 7:30 am the 1st Battalion was pinned down by artillery fire coming from north of Azeville. From 10:00 am to 3:00 pm, the shelling along with rifle and mortar fire was taking severe casualties on the 1st Battalion. They were then reinforced with Co. B, 359th Infantry of the 90th Division, which had advanced from the rear during the early morning hours. Company B stayed for two days and provided support in the fiercest fighting so far. That afternoon the 1st Battalion received a counterattack by an entire machine gun battalion on bicycles, but the 1st kept moving slowly forward. Company D then started firing its six 81 mm mortars with the assistance of the CP delivering 400 rounds into the enemy in about 10 minutes. The enemy firing then slowed, and many German bodies lay in front of the 1st Battalion. If this counter attack had succeeded, the Germans could have opened up a frontal assault all the way to Utah Beach. Sometime in the morning, Company C (Frank's Company) reached a road intersection about a half mile west of Azeville just to the west of an orchard and received an enemy barrage of shelling. Ironically a stone cross marked the intersection, and it was here that many of Company C were killed and wounded by the shelling and rifle fire. The cross, shown here, appears to be quite old, possibly a few hundred years.

Figure 117 Azeville Stone Cross

It is probable that the shelling came from just a few miles northeast of Azeville where there was a massive concrete German battery. At this location were four 105 mm guns that could reach Utah Beach but with poor accuracy at that range. The next day this battery was subjected to an extensive bombardment from Allied ships and then attacked by the 12th with flamethrowers. The garrison with at least 100 German soldiers then surrendered. (13)

Figure 118 Azeville Coastal Gun Battery

There is a reason to believe that Frank was killed early in the morning on June 8th. A letter dated July 28, 1944, from Al MacDonald to Dominic (Mannie) Costa stated, *"While in the lull in battle in France, I inquired as to how is Frank. One fellow, a corporal, stated he was alongside Frank when he was killed. When I heard this, I couldn't believe it, so I inquired further but still the same answer. I brooded on it something terrible as Frank was one of the best pals I ever had."*

Later in the same letter, he writes, *"I got a letter from another one of Franks pals today namely Tech. Sgt. Vito Santangelo. Like you, he inquired about him and as to what I knew. You see Frank was in his platoon, Vic being the platoon sergeant. We three were great buddies as we all had much in common. After a fierce day of fighting I saw Vic almost in tears, so I asked him what is the matter, to which he replied, I don't know where Frank is, I think he's missing. I sure got a funny feeling inside, a feeling I can't express. I couldn't believe it, but further inquiry brought out what I've already told you."*

Based on the above account it is believed that Frank was probably struck by rifle fire or shrapnel, which was fatal. The author visited Vic Santangelo in the year 2000 at his home in Fairport, NY. I asked Vic what he knew about Frank's death on June 8th. He told me that the rifle fire was horrendous coming from the German lines that morning and said he was struck in the left shoulder and removed by medics from the battlefield.

On the same day, June 8th, two of Frank's close friends were also killed, Corporal Bob Leonard, who was operating as a scout on Frank's squad and Sgt. Harry Newark. The next day Al MacDonald was hit by rifle fire and struck in the mouth taking out several teeth. He was evacuated to a hospital in England where he spent the next few months undergoing surgery and recuperating until being returned to the Platoon in September. It was only a few weeks when he was wounded again by shrapnel in the ankle and sent again to a hospital this time in France. He was not returned to action a second time.

Another letter providing details on the fateful day of June 8th was written to Mrs. Leonard, Bob Leonard's mother, on November 8, 1947, from Edmund F. Phillips, a soldier in Frank's squad. This letter in its entirety is provided in Appendix C. Edmund writes, *"The last I saw Bob he was acting as first scout and was telling our squad leader (Frank Brown), who was also killed, what he saw up ahead of him. Now that was when I was wounded and was evacuated to England. I later returned to the Company and learned about all the casualties we suffered that day which was over 2/3 of the Company, around 125 men. A fellow by the name of Crocker from Tennessee told me that Bob was killed alongside him, and it was so quick and sudden that there was no pain at all. Well, that is all I can tell you."*

Further information was obtained after Frank's sister, Mary, who wrote to Frank's platoon officer, 1st Lt. William A. Forbes. Lt. Forbes, in a letter dated March 5, 1945, wrote back, *"Our Company was in the vicinity of Montebourg in Normandy when the Germans threw a heavy counterattack at us. In this action, a large number of the company was lost. In this action Sgt. Brown displayed bravery and courage this is not found in the common man. It was indeed a thing to be remembered. After the action, we took again the ground we had lost and recovered the dead and wounded. This was on the 8th of June. I consider it a great honor to have fought beside your brother. I do hope you can find some small consolation in knowing that he died a brave man, and he was one of the finest men I have known."* This letter in its entirety can be found in Appendix D.

The battle on June 8th continued with the 3rd Battalion reaching Emondeville around noon with the 2nd Battalion on the left flank. There was intense machine gun fire from the hedgerows, which was gradually subdued by heroic efforts of the battalion. At this point, the 12th had pushed forward to the point where it passed the regiments on the right and left and as a result there was no flank protection. The CP was then moved into a group of buildings 1/2 mile west of Azeville, the same site that Company C had suffered so heavily that morning. However, the enemy spotted the location of the 12th CP and bombarded it for three hours. At 2:00 pm the CP was threatened with enemy assault and every man in the CP was organized into defense. The perimeter held with the assistance of counter-battery fire. The day finally ended at around dark at 9:30 pm with the taking of 100 German prisoners. (14)

In the days that followed, the 12th Regiment as part of the 4th Ivy Division continued fighting northward through the Cotentin Peninsula taking the critically vital port of Cherbourg on June 25, 1944. During the period of continuous action from June 6th to 28th, the division sustained over 5450 casualties and over 800 men killed. Along with the 2nd Armored Division, the 4th Division continued onto St. Lo on July 25, 1944. The 4th continued to attack through the hedgerow country, and along with the 2nd Armored Division, spearheaded the breakthrough that occurred at St. Lo on July 25,

1944. Exploiting the break in the German lines, the division continued the attack across France and on August 25, 1944, were along with the French 2nd Armored Division, the troops who earned the distinction of liberating Paris from four years of Nazi rule. Passing through the wildly applauding Parisians, the 4th left the victory parade and continued the pursuit of the Germans.

On September 11, 1944, a patrol from the 4th Infantry Division became the first Allied ground force to enter Germany. Fighting in the Siegfried Line followed. Mid-November found the division in the bloodiest battle of its history in the Hurtgen Forest. Fought in the cold rain and snow and a forest of pine and fir trees 150 feet in height, the Ivymen slugged it out yard-by-yard and day-by-day against determined German artillery and infantry. By early December, the division had fought through what now was a twisted mass of shrapnel-torn stumps and trees and had accomplished its mission. Casualties in the Hurtgen Forest were extensive.

With the Hurtgen Forest behind them, the division moved into a defensive position in Luxembourg and was soon to be engaged in the Battle of the Bulge. General George S. Patton wrote to Major General Raymond Barton of the 4th Infantry Division, *"Your fight in the Hurtgen Forest was an epic of stark infantry combat; but, in my opinion, your most recent fight from the 16th to the 26th of December, when, with a depleted and tired division, you halted the left shoulder of the German thrust into the American lines and saved the City of Luxembourg, and the tremendous supply establishments and road nets in that vicinity, it is the most outstanding accomplishment of yourself and your division."*

As the German push was halted in the Bulge, the Ivy Division resumed the attack and continued the pursuit back through the Siegfried Line at the same location it had crossed in September and fought across Germany as the war continued in the first four months of 1945. When the war ended on May 8, 1945, the 4th Infantry Division had participated in all the campaigns from the Normandy Beach through to Germany. Personnel of the Division during this period wear the five campaign stars for Normandy, Northern France, Rhineland, Ardennes, and Central Europe. Four Ivy Soldiers earned the Medal of Honor. The division suffered almost 22,000 battle casualties and over 34,000 total casualties during their eleven months fighting across Europe. On July 11, 1945, the Ivy Division returned to New York harbor and began preparing for the invasion of Japan. Fortunately, the war ended before that was required. (14)

2 Timothy 4:7-8 "I have fought the good fight, I have finished the race, I have kept the faith. Now there is in store for me the crown of righteousness which the Lord, the righteous judge, will award me on that day---and not only to me, but also to all who have longed for his appearing."

"****"

Chapter Fifteen

No Word
June 6 to August 6 1944

On the morning of June 6, 1944, a mother wrote her son, *"This morning I tuned in on the radio about eight o'clock and heard the news of the invasion. I listened in most all day. Tonight we all went to church at St. Peters, and there was a large crowd. Father McCoy said for all to pray more every day that world peace will come soon. We were thinking something was up as no one is getting mail from England. I pray and hope you won't have to leave England but if you do I pray God will watch over you and bring you back home safe again. I hope this will end the war sooner now. Dad, Alfred and Eleanor and all employees got a half hour off from work today to go to church. Billy said he prayed all the way up to the school this morning for you. Will close now and say my prayers and then get to bed. Love from us all and loads from Mother."*

The above letter was one of thirty-one letters written to Frank by his mother from May 26 to August 4, 1944. These letters that were never answered were all held somewhere by the army during this time-period. All 31 letters were returned at the same time in mid-August, and each was marked, *"Return to Sender, Deceased,"* signed, and dated by the platoon officer.

As the days continued in June, a long agonizing period occurred where mom, dad, and the family did not know anything about Frank. First, if indeed he was in the invasion, where was he at this time. Second, was he wounded or even worse captured by the Germans and now held as a prisoner of war. They could not believe the very worst had happened since they would have been notified within a few days if he had been severely injured or killed. No one feared, worried, agonized more than mom and her primary response was to pray throughout the day and write more letters at least every other day. Surely the letters must be getting through to him.

The following is a summarized log of these letters written desperately to her son, with the relentless thought, *my son, my son, where are you?*

May 23rd - *Bought 50 chickens, Billy left for school, washing machine broke.*

May 24th - *Billy mad, new pupil threw half his lunch away, hair appointment.*

May 26th - *Al & Billy to show, Billy dentist, Uncle Bill leaving the hospital.*

May 28th - *Planted potatoes and veggies, Al plowing, Billy & Mary sunburned.*

May 31st - *Model A Doodlebug needs a coil, Billy blowing your army whistle.*

June 2nd - *Mailing Jell-O chocolate bars, Al fixed wash machine, saw Uncle Bill.*

June 4th - *No one is getting mail from boys, Ray Regone shower June 9th.*

The day Frank was killed, June 8th, she wrote, *"Today I received your long waited letter. It was dated May 14th. For some reason, the mail has been delayed. I do hope you are getting my mail. We got a kick out your letter about the crow perched on the bald headed soldier. Frank, please write and ask for candy or whatever you want as I can't send you anything unless you ask for it. They ask Dad to show the line in your letter where it says what you request. They are pretty strict. Tonight Alfred, Billy and I went to the show and saw The Song of Bernadette. It was quite a sad picture. It is now almost twelve o'clock so must get to bed. Love from all at home. From you mother."*

Now there was no reason not to have hope since letters from Frank kept arriving due to the long transit time from England, so Mom kept on writing letters.

June 10th - *"Yesterday I received your letter of May 15th and this morning I received two dated 17th and 24th. Last night we were all down to Mannie Carli's hall to attend Ray Regone's shower. He received a lot of nice useful gifts. Mannie (Carli) was there and looks fairly good after what he went through. I will write Mary to get a movie film and take Rays wedding. He is getting married the 18th of June. Last night Raymond Longhany told Billy he had a girlfriend. Billy said I have two, but I have to find out which one is Catholic. HA! We got a kick out of that. Love from all, Mother."*

June 11th - *Went to Aunt Lucy's for dinner, Ralph Sperry in the infantry in Italy.*

June 13th - *Billy exams, nervous on spelling, hope you are not in fighting zone.*

June 15th - *Got three of your letters, Ed Longhany has a girl, passed driver test.*

June 16th - *Got your May 30th letter, school picnic, Dad & Al planting potatoes.*

June 18th - *Ray & Ella married 3:30 today. Mary took movie pictures.*

June 19th - *Pray you are not in the war zone. Billy out of school tomorrow.*

June 20th - *Billy good grades, now in 4th. How is your cold? Vic R in England.*

Frank's sister Mary wrote June 20th concerning conditions at home. *"Invasion is big news here. On the 6th, there was a blackout just before it was announced and I had an idea that it had started. Every day the latest reports are broadcasted through a loudspeaker on Main Street. There is a big bridge across Main Street, called a bond bridge with a bell on top of it and every time anyone buys a bond the bell is rung. Of course, mom and dad are quite worried about you but they are still receiving mail from you, and that is comforting. I don't worry anymore. I think that you are a pretty neat guy and can take care of yourself. So long for now and take care of yourself. Love, Your Sis, Mary."*

June 21st - *Got your May 31st ltr., hope you get furlough soon, Ed Longhany graduates.*

June 23rd - *Got your May 26th ltr., Billy got the second prize in health, a toothbrush.*

June 26th - *Not getting your mail, Billy & Chuckie went fishing, Dad to town.*

June 27th - *Not getting your mail, Billy no fish, Chuckie three fish, so Billy mad.*

The next letter mom wrote Frank started to show real concern for his welfare.

June 29th - *In paper Vic Santangelo wounded June 8th, now we know you are in a battle zone, thinking of you always, my heart is broken, praying God is watching over you.*

June 30th - *No mail, when I get into bed I think where is my Frank sleeping tonight. Hard to believe you are in the battle zone. I have you on my mind all the time and pray to God every day.*

Then on July 1, 1944, a letter was received from Pfc. Al MacDonald (Mac), with a Red Cross letterhead dated June 24, 1944. Al MacDonald was in Frank's squad and was severely wounded on June 9th, the day after Frank was killed. He was recovering now in a hospital in England and wrote this letter thinking that Frank's parents already had been notified of his death. As it turned out, this was the first notification of anything wrong and only resulted in disbelief and more confusion. Mac with good intentions was trying to express his grief in the loss of such a good friend and leader of his squad. Later Mac sincerely regretted sending this letter as he expressed to Frank's parents and others.

Al writes, *"Words cannot express my feelings on the recent loss of your son and my pal Frank. As you know, we had much in common therefore our friendship was a continual affair. Frank was a most conservative fellow and like myself, we both didn't smoke and drink. We found our pleasures in the movies of which we went but often. Our day would compose of a movie and ice cream, southern fried chicken and more ice cream. We sure did like our ice cream, and often we'd boast as to how much we could eat. I told him of a place in Hartford Conn. called the Highland Dairy where they had super sundaes and wagered Frank a bet that he couldn't eat one of their Steamboats. I was quickly accepted on this challenge, so time was to tell. It makes me sad to reminisce like this but how can I ever forget such a swell pal. Of how we often spoke of our plans and how we were both expected to visit one another. As he stated, I'll show you all around Le Roy to which I used to reply that won't take long. They come no better than Frank, and I'm saying this from a fellow speaking from the heart. He kept up exceptionally well on his religious duties, which was just another fine point about him. Yes, Frank and I had much in common and someday with your permission I'd like to meet the parents of this pal of mine. Frank left memories with me and the people in whom he came in contact. He was happy and carefree in life, and when the final whistle blew at the end of his day, I'm certain that he entered the Great Beyond with just as much enthusiasm and hope for the Future. Yes, Mr. and Mrs. Brown, he was indeed a fine young man. A pal of Franks, Al MacDonald."*

I remember this day well, a bright and sunny day on Saturday, July 1, 1944. The family was all home except for Mary, who was in Rochester working at Eastman Kodak. It was around noon, and the mailman had come with the morning mail. Mom would usually get the mail, and she would wait anxiously to see if there were any

171

letters from Frank. There had not been any letters for about two weeks now, the last being dated May 31st. We all gathered in the kitchen; that is Dad, Mom, Al, Eleanor and I for Mom to open the letter and read it. Since it was on a Red Cross letterhead, there was an obvious concern. When my Mom read that first line, *"Words cannot express my feelings on the recent loss of your son and my pal Frank,"* she burst out in tears with *"Oh my God, Oh my God!"* My father was smoking a pipe and threw it across the kitchen floor hitting it so hard it broke into two pieces. My brother Al started to cry and ran out the back door and down the field past the red barn. Eleanor tried to comfort mom in total shock of what had just been made known. I just stood there, a boy of almost nine years, shocked and just not knowing what to do in such grief, which I had never experienced before in my life. I'm not sure of the rest of that fateful day but what I do know is that my parents could not completely believe that Frank was dead since there was no official confirmation from the War Department.

Not having any confirmation, Frank's dad immediately contacted the Red Cross to see what they could find out. I imagine there were hundreds of inquiries at this time because of the very high causality rate in Europe. I believe as a result of this request Frank's parents received a Western Union telegram, dated July 6th, stating, *"Name of Staff Sergeant Frank W. Brown does not appear on casualty lists received in War Department. Period. Investigation being made. Period. You will be notified upon receipt of a report. Period. Adj. General."* This reply did give his parents more hope that he was not dead but recovering in a hospital or maybe a prisoner of war. If he was in a hospital were his wounds so severe that he could not write or worse yet was he a prisoner of war and being mistreated. So mom started her letter writing again, still with the agonizing thought, **my son, my son, where are you?**

July 14th - *My dear son, we still don't get any mail from you. We are all praying and hope you are safe somewhere. We are hoping Mac is mistaken. Everyone tells us not to give up. We are all upset thinking of you every minute.*

July 18th - *No mail from you or news from War Dept. We are all praying. We are well at home but are all worried about you. Mac hasn't written anymore. Vic wounded in hospital.*

July 22nd - *No mail from you or War Dept. Almost everyone tells us not to believe in Mac's letter. We are all hoping and praying you are safe somewhere. Pray war will be over soon. Vic Regone somewhere in France.*

July 25th - *One month ago got Mac's letter. No word from War Dept. but still have hope. Dad went to Red Cross, and they will investigate again. We believe you are taken a prisoner and pray you are taken care of.*

July 28th - *No news, miss your letters so much. Pat Fallon has not heard from her husband since D-Day.*

Aug 1st - *Wrote to Mac but no reply. Uncle Bill papered living room and kitchen; we do not feel like doing it after Mac's letter.*

Aug 4th - *Mary got a letter from Mac saying he saw Frank fall on the battlefield but not sure living or not. We believe now you are wounded and in a hospital. Your mother is praying all she can and family also. We hope you will recover soon and will write to us. Billy is going to summer school a few weeks and likes it.*

Then the Western Union telegram arrived on August 6, 1944. The telegram, of course, eliminated all hope of Frank being alive in a hospital or a prisoner of war.

Figure 82 Telegram on Frank's Death

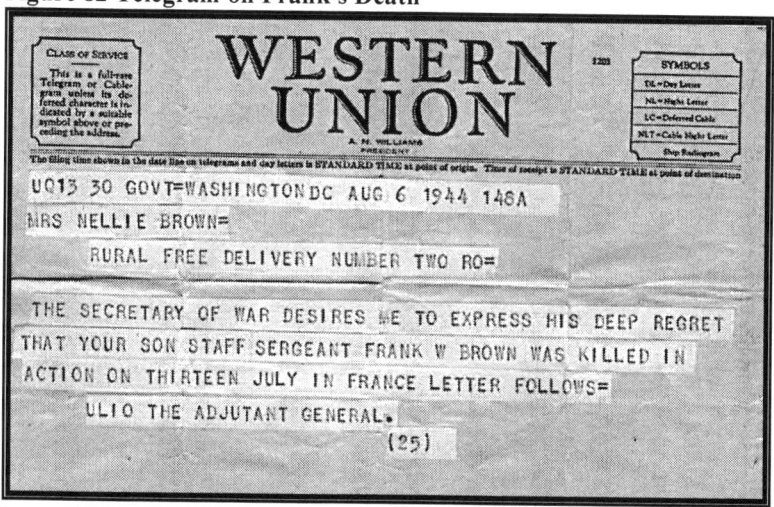

```
WESTERN UNION

UO13 30 GOVT=WASHINGTON DC AUG 6 1944 146A
MRS NELLIE BROWN=
   RURAL FREE DELIVERY NUMBER TWO RO=

THE SECRETARY OF WAR DESIRES ME TO EXPRESS HIS DEEP REGRET
THAT YOUR SON STAFF SERGEANT FRANK W BROWN WAS KILLED IN
ACTION ON THIRTEEN JULY IN FRANCE LETTER FOLLOWS=
   ULIO THE ADJUTANT GENERAL.
                    (25)
```

I recall my mother being grief stricken. She called her sister Lucy who immediately came over to comfort her. I had a difficult time seeing my mom in tears and remember going out of the house to my swing hung from the apple tree near the front yard. Aunt Lucy was at this time also dealing with the grief of the loss of her son Richard Longhany. Richard was a Navy gunner on a merchant ship in a convoy crossing the Atlantic, which was torpedoed on the night of February 23, 1943, as noted previously in this book. His parents were notified on April 22, 1943, that he was missing at sea. His parents also were not officially notified until February 24, 1944, a year after his death. What a long, long time his parents waited not knowing if he survived as a prisoner of war. So I'm confident that these two grief-stricken sisters were a comfort to each other at this very trying time. I always remember Aunt Lucy as a very kind and caring woman who displayed a concerned and anxious look on her face. I don't believe a person can live a grief experience such as this without it affecting them in many different ways.

Frank's father took the grief in a different manner. He was a hard working, very kind man with strong character. However as a man, he had trouble handling grief, and it showed right away in anger. He was angry at the War Department for taking so long in getting a reply. He was angry when they found out the date of death, as called out on the August 6th telegram, was not June 13th but instead June 8th. He was angry when he read in the newspapers that many times the men were not protected by tanks or armored vehicles but would have to expose themselves completely to the enemy to gain ground. He knew the 4th Division was originally designed as a rolling armored division where the tanks and half-tracs were embedded in the various companies, but this changed in late 1943. He was angry at the President and Congress for being responsible for the greatest nation in the world being unprepared for the war and suffering such a defeat at Pearl Harbor. This anger was expressed many a time at the supper table, and it tempered me a lot to not even question or challenge him.

Shortly after the August 6th telegram, I remember being in the town of Le Roy with my father riding in our 1936 Chevy four-door sedan. We pulled up in front of the Le Roy Municipal Building. In front of the building was a large billboard, around 8 feet high and 18 feet long. On it were the names of WWII Le Roy soldiers, each painted on a 2 by 12-inch board, nailed to the billboard. Those killed had a gold star by the name. My father left the car with a pair of pliers and tore off Frank's name, rushed back to the car and quickly put it under the drivers floor mat. I was shocked and thought we are in trouble, and the police will soon be after us. That did not happen of course, and I never told anyone about what happened that day. That was my father's way of handling his grief.

Letters were now starting to come in expressing condolences and sympathy for my parent's loss. Vic Santangelo's parents sent a letter as early as July 7th, apparently hearing from their wounded son in an England hospital that Frank was killed. Then a letter from Mrs. Martha Leonard (Bob Leonard's mother) dated July 12th, where she says she was notified on June 26th that Bob was killed in action on June 8th. Two days later a letter came confirming the date of June 8th. Mrs. Leonard writes, *"I have prayed so hard that the boys might be saved, but God wanted them, and I've tried to think during these past days that maybe he has been spared lots of suffering from the year to come. I am thinking that Bob and Frank are where no one will ever hurt them again."*

Then there were letters from people that Frank's mom did not even know but offered a respectful insight into the character of her son. One letter was written by Toni Pennello, a cousin of Vic Santangelo and pen pal of Al MacDonald. She writes, *"Please do not think of me as forward in writing to you. If this letter is an imposition and it distresses you, I'm truly sorry. My name is Antoinette Pennello, and I am Vito Santangelo's cousin. I am also a friend of Alan MacDonald. These two boys had the wonderful fortune of knowing your son's true friendship and comradeship. Each one of their letters made some mention of Frank Brown or Sgt. Brown as they called him. They spoke so well of your son--his sincerity, his honesty, his leadership, his great love for all mankind, his thoughtfulness, and consideration of others and his quiet humor. He with all these fine qualities did much to enlighten the hardships of their army life and to ease the pain of separation from their loved ones. Vito and Mac have always given Frank as an example of the perfect American boy, always a gentleman and a fine credit to the upbringing his mother and father gave him. These two boys lost a dear friend in your son, something that time alone can take care of. But to you, my heart goes out in a deep and with sincere sympathy. Even the long span of the coming years can nowhere ease the pain and suffering that is yours today. I pray that God with all this merciful tenderness will give you the strength to go on and lead a happy and full life. I know that Frank would want it that way."* I don't believe any better words could have been written.

Mannie Costa, Frank's brother-in-law, wrote Al MacDonald also inquiring of Frank's death and asking for any particulars that might help to ease the pain of loss to his parents. Mac responded in a letter dated July 28th, expressing his grief at the loss of such a good friend and his remorse in sending that letter of June 24th to Frank's parents. He writes, *"I have been thinking a lot about Frank lately as only last nite I dreamed he was alive and well. Somehow I can't believe he is dead, even if I was told so by quite a few fellows in his platoon. When I wrote Frank's parents, I was in a sad mood thinking of Frank. I just came to the hospital and was feeling all round miserable. I wrote to his people thinking it the best thing to do, but now I realize I did the worst thing ever. My telling his parents was something I should never have done as I caused them a lot of grief. I trust in God that those fellows were wrong even as convincing as they seemed."* I believe Mac carried this regret with himself for a long time and only after he met Frank's parents in 1945 was he able to start to ease his pain of loss and his regret in writing. Mac remained a friend for many years afterward.

Another surprise letter was received from a Mrs. Thielman from Buffalo, NY, dated September 4, 1944. Mrs. Thielman was the mother of Eleanor Thielman, who was a grade school pen pal of Franks for two and a half years. When a letter Eleanor wrote in June came back marked deceased and signed by the platoon officer, they knew that Frank was killed but did not know any details. Eleanor wanted to go and see Frank's parents right away, but her mom said they should not do so since Frank's parents were very grieved and would not want any visitors now. So the September 4th letter was sent informing Frank's parents of who they were and how Eleanor had exchanged with Frank cards, birthday gifts, and valentines. Eleanor had received many lovely gifts, several pictures and kept corresponding faithfully until mid-August, when she received her last letter returned marked deceased. Mrs. Thielman writes, *"We all were so sorry as we all felt as though Frank was a dear friend, and we were waiting for the day when we could meet him. Please accept the deepest sympathy from my family and me and do not think we are too nervy in writing. O course we all prayed for him."*

Then a letter came from Virginia MacInnis, the girl that Frank had never met but corresponded with frequently. She had a special place in Frank's heart since her photos were found in his wallet when he was killed on the battlefield. He also had a larger photo always hanging above his cot in his barracks. Virginia writes in a letter dated September 11, 1944, *"I find it very hard starting this letter because I don't know quite what to say. I know that nothing I can say will ease your sorrow over Frank. You must miss him terribly, and I can realize how you feel because I feel the same way. I never knew Frank in the sense that most people mean when they speak of knowing someone, but I feel that I knew him as well as I could possibly know anyone. I wrote to him for two years, and occasionally I would read his letters to my family, and they too thought a great deal of Frank. That is going some for my Dad because he usually resents any attention paid to his precious daughters. To me, Frank was a wonderful person. He had ideals far above those of most ordinary people and was extremely fond of his mother, as you know. I remember once I sent him a birthday card and he wrote back and told me how badly he felt because he had forgotten your birthday. All these things you know better than I Mrs. Brown, but it helps me to tell you how I felt about Frank and how I miss his letters so. The thing we must do now is pray, for only with the help of God, will we ever see the finish of this war."* This letter was the first of several letters written between Virginia and Frank's mom, which helped to ease the pain and loss each of them felt.

Vic Santangelo, who was wounded on June 8th and recuperating in a hospital in England, could not write Frank's parents at first due to the grief he was experiencing. In July, he was returned to the 12th Infantry, as Company C technical sergeant. He was again exposed to battle day after day. In September, Vic starting writing letters, first to Mrs. Leonard, then to Frank's sister Mary, and finally to Frank's parents dated September 16th. He writes, *"I ask you, first of all, to forgive me for not having written to you before this and express my deepest sympathies for your great loss. But you see I found it too difficult to even try to express my absolute feelings in a letter. I have just received your card and letter. It was delayed because of my moving about so. I want to thank you all for thinking of me. I have been back with the company now since the 20th of July and thank God everything is all right with me. Allen is still in the hospital, and I pray it won't be necessary for him to come back here. Between him and I, we miss our best buddy more than anyone will ever know and the sorrow and heartbreaks we boys must witness daily. The world will little know and appreciate the grand fine boys that have given their lives for it. Only the individuals as you well know, you who have lost your best. I pray to God daily out here, as I know all of you at home do, that this awful war would end soon. If God will grant me the grand opportunity to go home again, I will never, never stop being thankful. If my wish is granted, I want to see you all again and talk to you. Please write again if you care too. I will try to answer as soon as possible. Please forgive me again and also for not writing sooner."*

Al MacDonald was returned to the 12th Regiment, 1st Battalion, Company C in September and was wounded again a few weeks later in early October 1944 by a piece of shrapnel in his foot. He wrote from an army hospital in France on October 8th, *"I'm once again a victim of a wound, this time, it being a piece of shrapnel in the foot. Don't know how bad it is at present but I do believe that I'll be kept in for some time...Met Vic while back in the company and confidentially he looks all worn out. War sure does age a person especially the infantry."*

On October 17th, they received another letter from Vic Santangelo saying he was somewhere in Germany. He writes, *"The other day I answered Mac's letter which he had written to me from the hospital. He seems to be getting along fairly well, and I pray it will not be necessary to enter this fight again for him. Believe me, when I say, Mrs. Brown, that I can truly understand your feelings after such a great loss. For I, myself miss him very much."*

Mrs. Leonard shared a letter she received from Vic Santangelo dated November 29, 1944, somewhere in Germany. He writes, *"In answer to some of your questions I might attempt to answer them so you may understand me. Frank and Harry Newark both went the same as your Bob, no suffering believe me. Harry was the boy that was married in Trenton while we were stationed in Ft. Dix. Allen McDonald is now back with the company after being out for quite some time because of wounds received. I hate to see those boys come back, Mrs. Leonard--hate to see them having to come back to this horrible mess. I pray they wouldn't have had too. The weather here has been something awful and hindering our advance some. We have seen our first snow in Germany already and are now sweating out the rest of the winter, so to speak. It is difficult to describe and say what one wants to in a letter, Mrs. Leonard. Our constant prayers are for this to all end soon, for we are tired, very tired. No one in all this world will be happier when it ends, than the boys in the foxholes on the front lines. The world little realizes or will ever know what goes on here. Perhaps it is best they don't."* My parents must have felt some consolation after reading this letter and previous ones that at least Frank did not have to suffer from the battle fatigue or other worst consequences of the war.

The date of Frank's death continued to confuse the family since they heard from the War Department that it occurred on June 13th, but his platoon buddies were reporting June 8th. Frank's parents received a letter from Vic Santangelo dated December 19th, which helped to confirm the date. He writes, *"Mrs. Brown I know it is best to try to forget your sorrows and perhaps I shouldn't bring back the aching memories by discussing it. But for your sake and if it will help to relieve the ache in your heart I will and can tell you that Frank did not suffer, nor did he die in a hospital on the dates mentioned by you. He died on the battlefield as the true grand soldier he was. The date was the 8th of June. Now for his sake Mrs. Brown and I know he'd want it that way, please try to alleviate your mind and try to put yourself at ease. I know better then to say try to forget for if I can't how can I possibly ask you to do that? My sincerest wishes to you and the rest of the family. How is the little fellow of the family? I can't think of his name just now. May God bless you all. Sincerely, Vic"*

Philippians 4:6-7 "Do not be anxious about anything, but in everything by prayer and petition, with thanksgiving, present your requests to God. And the peace of God, which transcends all understanding, will guard your hearts and your minds in Christ Jesus."

"****"

Chapter Sixteen

Coming Home
1944 to 1948

The fall of 1944 was a difficult one for Frank's family in coming to the full reality of Frank's battlefield death. I remember when returning home from school, I would have my milk and homemade cookie and witness my mom in tears as she started to prepare supper. I did not know a person could shed that many tears. Other members of the family did not show their sorrow as much, more in a silent containment. My father continued to express anger about anything with the war effort or President Franklin D. Roosevelt. There were the occasional letters from Frank's girlfriend, Virginia MacInnis, Vic Santangelo's girl Rose, Mrs. Martha Leonard, Vic or Mac's mothers, or from Vic and Mac themselves. There were joy and sorrow expressed in these letters from very caring people now very weary of what seemed like an unending war.

On December 7, 1944, Frank's mom sent a letter to the Adjutant General regarding the burial of Frank. A reply from the Office of the Quartermaster General was received on January 2, 1945, stating the following:

"*The official report received in this office reveals that the remains of your son were reverently and properly interred in the U. S. Military Cemetery #1, St. Mere Eglise, France, Plot D, Row 4, Grave 77, with a Catholic ceremony conducted at the grave by an Army Chaplain. The cemetery is well cared for and under the immediate supervision of our military authorities. The grave is properly recorded, and a temporary marker with an appropriate inscription thereon has 6een erected. I wish to extend to you my sincere sympathy in the loss of your son.*"

It's somewhat ironic that on the same day, a letter was received from the War Department, Adjutant General's Office, Demobilized

Personnel Records Branch, dated January 2, 1945, concerning his parent's inquiry of Frank's death. The letter states:

"*Reference is made to your letters of 7 and 12 December 1944, in which you request further information in connection with the death of your son, Staff Sergeant Frank W. Brown, Army serial number 32131532. I can fully understand your desire to learn as much as possible concerning the death of your son. Additional records now available show that your son was killed in action at Montebourg, France, on 13 June 1944, while participation in the occupation of the Normandy coast. He had participated in this engagement since 6 June 1944. I wish that I were able to furnish you with additional information, but no further particulars relative thereto, were given. At a later day in another communication, you will be advised regarding the Army serial number on the Purple Heart certificate.*"

On June 9, 1945, a letter was received from the War Department, Adjutant General's Office providing more information on Frank's death concerning details of location and confirming the date. Unfortunately, the letter provided more confusing information.

"*Your letter of inquiry concerning your son, Staff Sergeant Frank W. Brown has been forwarded from overseas. Your desire to know the circumstances attending the death of your son is most understandable. An additional report has been received in the War Department, which discloses that Sergeant Brown was killed by shrapnel in the vicinity of Montebourg, France, on 13 June 1944. The report did not disclose whether your son received the last sacraments.*"

So again the location and date were in conflict with what had been reported by Frank's platoon buddies, Vic, and Mac. The error was carried all the way through to the grave marker, which today shows the date of death as June 13, 1944. It is true that there were so many deaths the first few days of the invasion that bodies were hastily recovered from the battlefield and transported to a makeshift gravesite. The records were sometimes delayed by several weeks. There must have been an error on Frank's date of death, since his buddy, Bob Leonard, was killed the same day but his mother was notified within two weeks, and the location was correct.

When Frank's body was recovered from the battlefield, an Army truck took it to a farmer's field, which was just bought from a local French farmer by the Quarter Master Corps. Since it was so close to St. Mere Eglise, it was called St. Mere Eglise Cemetery. There were so many casualties on D-Day and the days that followed, that the bodies could not be buried immediately but were laid on stretchers in the field until burial. More American soldiers were killed the first three days of the invasion, then in the entire Iraq and Afghan war from 2003 to 2014.

Figure 83 St. Mere Eglise Cemetery

There were not enough American soldiers to bury the dead, so to accomplish the burial task, recently captured German prisoners were used. They were supervised and guarded by MP's while performing this task and graves were dug by hand since there was no excavating equipment available. The body would be covered in a blanket or if available placed in a white cotton bag although most of the soldiers were buried in their uniforms.

Soldiers were required to wear two identical identification tags nicknamed Dog Tags. When a soldier was recovered from the battlefield, one Dog Tag would be taken from the soldier's body for notification and the second remained with the body for burial identification. Before burial, any personal effects and one dog tag were removed and put in a bag marked with the name and serial number. If you want to witness the real horror of war in its aftermath, then view a YouTube video of a scene taken by the Army with a 16 mm movie camera at the St. Mere Eglise Cemetery on June 18, 1944, just ten days after Frank was killed and buried there. The video is very realistic in showing several bodies being buried and about 100 German POW's providing the hand labor. Go to YouTube, "https://www.youtube.com/watch?v=PeYTt-5cL8U"or "Cimetière / Cemetery - Sainte-Mère-Eglise - 18/06/1944 - DDay-Overlord".

Figure 121 French Women Placing Flowers on Graves

Wooden stakes were placed on the grave with the soldier's serial number. The picture shows French women placing flowers on the graves shortly after burial, which they faithfully perform to this day. Several months later the stakes were replaced with a white wooden marker with the soldier's name and serial number.

On September 9, 1947, a letter was sent from a Private Ted Liska to Mrs. Martha Leonard concerning a request she made about her son Bob's gravesite at the St. Mere Eglise Military Cemetery No 1. He wrote a very emotional letter on his duties at the cemetery and his devotion to his fallen buddies and their families.

"I am an Honor Guard here at St. Mere Eglise Cemetery No. 2. I used to be in Co. D, 12th Inf. Regt. 4th Div. I landed here on D-Day at Utah Beach. I was pretty lucky for I was wounded in the right thigh at Mortain, France on Aug. 10, 1944. I trained with your son Leonard. We went together to Fort Pierce Fla. for Scout & Raiders School. He slept in the same tent with me. I remember one day he went to one of your relatives who lives near Ft. Pierce. He brought us back a lot of oranges and grapefruit. I haven't been home since 1943. Here at the cemetery, I know at least 200 or 300 of the boys. I feel like a big brother to all of them. I know a lot of families can't come here to see this beautiful Cemetery, so I took it upon myself to try to do a good deed for these boys who I know so well and fought along side of me during combat. I hope you like the snapshots I took. If there should be anything else I can do for you, please let me know. I would be glad to do it. This is just a little way of mine of trying to do one good deed every day. We have here at our Cemetery 4816 soldiers, and at least 1000 of these came from the 4th Div. I expect to be going to the States in 48. Well, so long

Mrs. Leonard. May God Bless you. I remain, one of your son's Buddies, Private Ted Liska, 36304456."

Mrs. Leonard sent a copy of Private Liska's letter to Frank's mom and soon after she received photos of Frank's grave at St. Mere Eglise Cemetery. This was the first time she saw the gravesite and must have provided comfort to her.

Figure 84 Frank's Grave Marker at St. Mere Eglise Cemetery

It was at this time that Frank's parents received a letter from the War Department, the Office of the Quartermaster General, dated September 18, 1947. The letter references the location of the burial plot for Frank as follows:

S/Sgt. Frank W. Brown, 32 131 532
Plot D, Row 4, Grave 77,
United States Military Cemetery
St. Mere Eglise #1, France
Mr. Jacob Brown, Rural Free Delivery #2, Le Roy, NY

The people of the United States, through the Congress, have authorized the disinterment and final burial of the heroic dead of World War II. The Quartermaster General of the Army has been entrusted with this sacred responsibility to the honored dead. The records of the War Department indicate that you may be the nearest relative of the above named deceased, who gave his life in the service of his country.

The letter provided a pamphlet on the Disposition of World War II Armed Forces Dead and said they are invited to express the wishes as to the disposition of the remains of the deceased by completing a form on the Request for Disposition of Remains. Frank's parents selected Option 2, which was the return to the family the remains for burial by the family or in a US military cemetery. They were advised not to make any funeral arrangements until further notification.

Figure 85 St. Mere Eglise Cemetery #1

Next a letter from Private Teddy Liska dated March 20, 1948, sent to Mrs. Leonard, and provided more information on the status of the St. Mere Eglise Cemetery. *"I have some news for you and*

185

Mrs. Brown. *They closed St Mere Eglise No. 1 and No. 2 Cemeteries Sunday, March 7th. They are already working on No. 1, and Mrs. Brown can expect her son home sometime in May, I hope. They won't start here in No. 2 until April so Bob won't be coming home until June or July. They had a big ceremony when they closed the cemetery. All the people from St. Mere Eglise were here to say goodbye to the soldiers who gave their lives so that they could be free. I am getting along fine, and I hope you are too. May God bless you and your family. I remain, Your adopted son, Teddy."*

We should indeed be proud of our country for taking such good care of the military cemeteries in Europe. Since many families wanted their loved ones returned to the states, about 60%, they closed several temporary military cemeteries. St. Mere Eglise No. 1 & 2 was two of these cemeteries that were closed. Those left in the cemetery were moved to the Normandy American Cemetery and Memorial near Colleville-sur-Mer, France, which overlooks Omaha Beach. The St. Mere Eglise No. 1 & 2 contained around 14,000 American soldiers including Brigadier General Teddy Roosevelt who was on the staff of the 4th Infantry Division and at age 56, landed on the first wave at Utah Beach. General Teddy Roosevelt died of a heart attack on July 12, 1944, and was buried at St. Mere Eglise and later moved to the Normandy American Cemetery.

Regarding Frank's personal effects, a letter notified his parents on January 17, 1945, from the Kansas City Quartermaster Depot, Army Effects Bureau the following:

"The Army Effects Bureau has received from overseas some personal property of your son, S/Sgt. Frank W. Brown. I regret to advise that included among your son's effects is a photo case, which is damaged, apparently by mold. Also, the photos, which it contains. To make proper disposition of this property, it is necessary that we have certain information regarding your son's family. I would like to know whether he was married and, if so, the name and address of his widow. Please mail your reply as this will accelerate delivery of the property."

A few weeks later a small package was received of his personal effects. Among these effects was a water-damaged billfold within which were the photos of Virginia MacInnis, the girl he corresponded with on a frequent basis for almost two years.

Figure 124 Pictures of Virginia MacInnis in Frank's Wallet

Since these were the photos he had in his possession, when he was on the battlefield, she sure must have had a very special place in his heart. If he would have survived the war, one wonders if they would have married, had children and what legacy they would have left.

Figure 125 Le Roy Gazette News Article

Body of Le Royan Arrives Tonight

The body of Staff Sergeant Frank W. Brown, 27, son of Mr. and Mrs. Jacob Brown of the Le Roy-Pavilion road, will arrive in Le Roy this evening at 6:30 and will be met at the B & O station by an honor guard of Legionnaires and escorted to the Steuber Funeral Home, Trigon Park.

Funeral services for the war hero who met his death on July 13, 1944, during the invasion of France, will be held at nine o'clock Saturday morning from St. Joseph's Church. Burial will be in St. Francis Cemetery.

Flags will be flown at half-mast throughout the village Friday and Saturday in tribute to the native Le Royan.

Military Funeral For S-Sgt. Brown

Military funeral services for Staff Sgt. Frank W. Brown were held Saturday morning from St. Joseph's Church with the Rev. J. Stanly Ormsby officiating.

S-Sgt. Brown was escorted by a color guard of Legionnaires of the Botts-Fiorito Post, No. 576, from the Steuber Funeral Home to the church and to interment in St. Francis Cemetery.

The color guard was composed of Harold Wright, James Baldwin, Janssen, William McMahon, Jack Fagan and Ellsworth Mooney, commanded by Charles Felt.

Honor bearers were Gerald Platt, James Perrone, Henry Zimmerman, John Green, Louis P. Brady, Jr., and Louis Davis.

M-Sgt. Le Roy Baker served as the military escort for S-Sgt. Brown from Schenectady to Le Roy and remained here for 48 hours. He presented the American Flag to Mrs. Jacob Brown, mother of S-Sgt. Brown, for her son's valor and heroism in war, at the cemetery.

S-Sgt. Brown was killed June 13th, 1944, in the invasion of Normandy, France. He was awarded the Purple Heart posthumously.

Surviving are his parents, Mr. and Mrs. Jacob Brown of the Le Roy-Pavilion highway; two sisters, Mrs. D. A. Costa and Miss Mary Jo Brown; and two brothers, Alfred C. and William Brown, all of Le Roy.

Frank's remains were returned in mid-May 1948 to the USA. As was the standard procedure, his body was accompanied by Master Sergeant L. E. Baker, who was stationed at the Schenectady General Depot, 1309 A. S. U. Edt. #2 in Schenectady, NY. On May 20th, the body was picked up at the Le Roy railroad station and transported to the Steuber Funeral Home to lie in state for one day, Friday, May 21st.

Figure 126 Frank's Funeral Card

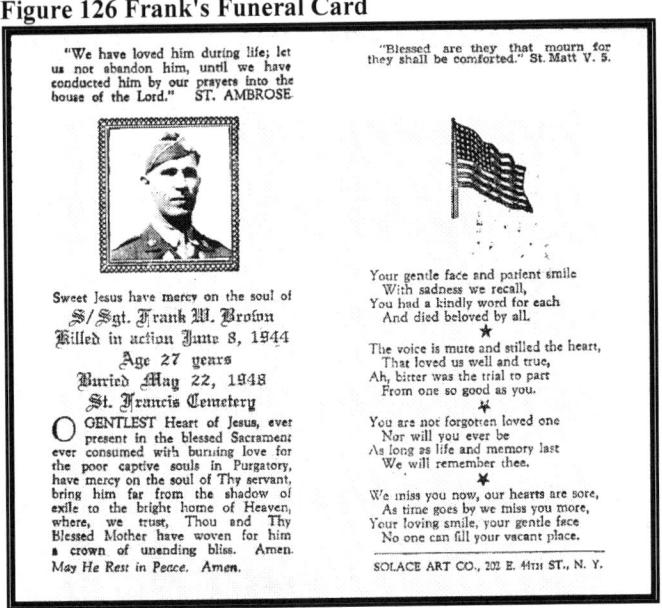

"We have loved him during life; let us not abandon him, until we have conducted him by our prayers into the house of the Lord." ST. AMBROSE

"Blessed are they that mourn for they shall be comforted." St. Matt V. 5.

Sweet Jesus have mercy on the soul of
S/Sgt. Frank W. Brown
Killed in action June 8, 1944
Age 27 years
Buried May 22, 1948
St. Francis Cemetery

O GENTLEST Heart of Jesus, ever present in the blessed Sacrament ever consumed with burning love for the poor captive souls in Purgatory, have mercy on the soul of Thy servant, bring him far from the shadow of exile to the bright home of Heaven, where, we trust, Thou and Thy Blessed Mother have woven for him a crown of unending bliss. Amen.
May He Rest in Peace. Amen.

Your gentle face and patient smile
With sadness we recall,
You had a kindly word for each
And died beloved by all.
★
The voice is mute and stilled the heart,
That loved us well and true,
Ah, bitter was the trial to part
From one so good as you.
★
You are not forgotten loved one
Nor will you ever be
As long as life and memory last
We will remember thee.
★
We miss you now, our hearts are sore,
As time goes by we miss you more,
Your loving smile, your gentle face
No one can fill your vacant place.

SOLACE ART CO., 202 E. 41TH ST., N. Y.

The author remembers the day since he got the day off from school. My father was asked if they wanted to verify the remains as those of Frank by using his dental records. Frank's parents choose not to have this done and made a request that taps not be played at the gravesite since it would be too difficult to bear.

Saturday, May 22nd, the family with many area relatives and friends gathered at the funeral home and then in procession moved to St. Joesph's Church where a burial mass was conducted. Afterward, the procession proceeded down Main Street with the color guard walking in front. I was so impressed with the color guard and noticed that the flag bearer was my present math teacher, Mr. James Perrone, who also served in WWII as a Navy PBY pilot. Those on the street that sunny Saturday morning would come to attention in reverence as the procession passed. At St. Francis Cemetery the family and relatives gathered around the burial site, which was reserved for Frank's parents and grandparents. The color guard fired blanks from their rifles as a final tribute to one of their own and the flag on the coffin was folded and given to Frank's mother.

Figure 127 M/Sgt. Baker, Mom & Dad

Figure 128 Flag Presented to Mom

The final chapter was now completed. As they were leaving the burial site notice was given to the tombstone, which displayed the incorrect date of Frank's death, June 13, 1944. Yes, we do live in an imperfect world.

Figure 129 Tombstone at St. Francis Cemetery

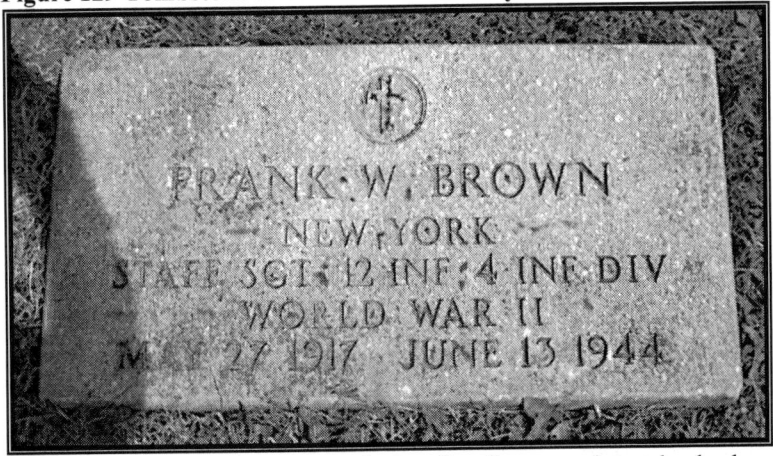

Finally, Frank's parents and the family members had closure with the return of Frank's body. Contact was kept with Frank's buddies Vic Santangelo and Al MacDonald through the coming years. Vic, battle weary, returned to the USA on a furlough in February 1945 and married his love Rose in Rochester, NY. On the ship crossing the Atlantic, he found his buddy Al MacDonald in the hospital section of the ship and what a surprise that was for both of them. Al (Mac) was still immobilized by the foot wound and was transferred to a VA hospital in Rome, NY. Vic and Rose visited Al in the hospital so Al could meet Rose. They did quite a bit of reminiscing covering the three plus years that they knew each other, and both were still trying to adjust to the loss of their best pal, Frank. Shortly after, Vic was sent back to join Company C in Germany until the war in Europe ended on May 8, 1945. It was called V-E Day that marked the acceptance by the Allies of Nazi Germany's unconditional surrender of its armed forces. Vic wrote to Mrs. Brown on May 23rd,

"I'm so glad to have heard from you, since the last time I wrote. So many things have happened, the best, of course, being that the war over here finally has ended, thank God. The day we heard the good news, it was almost unbelievable but realistically true. I hope with the help of God the rest of the world will come to its senses also. As I stand, I figure on having a good chance on the Army's discharge plans. I honestly hope and pray my dreams will come true. Imagine how excited Rose is! I'm keeping my fingers crossed. God Bless you all, Love, Vic."

1 Thessalonians 4:16-18 "For the Lord himself will come down from heaven, with a loud command, with the voice of the archangel and with the trumpet call of God, and the dead in Christ will rise first. After that, we who are still alive and are left will be caught up together with them in the clouds to meet the Lord in the air. And so we will be with the Lord forever. Therefore, encourage each other with these words."

"****"

Epilogue

Frank's father died in June 1963 at the age of 72. He was a loving father to Frank and in time came to terms with Frank's death in the service he gave to his country. Frank's mother, Nellie, always spoke of her son with the utmost admiration and always had that place of sorrow in her heart for her first born. She died on April 12, 1995, at the age of 98, as the oldest Gold Star Mother in Genesee County, New York. Her life displayed a religious, forever kind and patient person with a constant uplifting attitude. Although the death of her son left a lasting ache in her heart, she approached life every day with joy.

Mannie Costa returned from the war in 1945 and worked for the Jell-O Company for a few years and then opened his own electrical service business, which he operated for several years. They had two boys and two girls. Frank's sister Mary married Robert Morgan in 1951. He also was a veteran of the 82nd Airborne in WWII, and they had one boy and five girls. Frank's brother Al never married and lived with his mother at the Le Roy homestead his entire life.

Frank's parents and the author visited Vic and Rose Santangelo in Rochester, NY on several occasions. They had two girls, Janet, and Linda that they adored. Vic became an employee of the US Post Office after the war. The author's last visit with him was just two years before he died in 2002. With reluctance, I asked him if he knew the particulars of Frank's death. Normally WWII soldiers do not like to talk about their wartime experience since it was just too painful for them. I wanted to honor that so I did not press him on details of that fateful day, June 8th. He did say that he was separated from Frank, and the rifle fire was horrendous when he was shot through the left shoulder. The author became a writing pal of Vic, and since he liked to read, he sent him several spiritual books.

Al MacDonald married after the war and worked in the US Post Office in Norwich, CN. He would visit Frank's parents every few years and in the summer of 1956, the author and his brother Al visited Mac and his wife Millie, now with their newborn baby boy. Mac was deeply affected by the war and showed a constant manner of nervousness. What these men went through in seeing the destruction and loss of life before them would have a significant effect on anyone. Nowadays they call it PSD but then it was called "shell shock." Time would calm their spirit, but they would never get over what they witnessed.

In December 2003, the author's relatives in Le Roy notified him that there was an article in the Le Roy Pennysaver titled, "A Soldier's Sacrifice Remembered". Lynne Belluscio, Town of Le Roy and village historian and the Director of the Le Roy Historical Society wrote it. Lynne wrote in the article that a Mrs. Eleanor Peinkofer from Buffalo, N. Y. was recently cleaning her attic when she came across letters she received from a pen pal in the army in WWII. His name was Frank W. Brown, and hers was Eleanor Thielman. Mrs. Peinkofer and her husband Joe decided to visit Le Roy to find Frank's gravesite. After arriving, they found the cemetery and through the help of another visitor found Frank's grave. They were urged to visit the Le Roy House and Jell-O Museum where they could find the local historian, Lynne Belluscio. The result of the visit was a news article in the Pennysaver which when noticed by local relatives, led the author to contact Mrs. Peinkofer.

On June 4, 2004, the author visited Eleanor (Thielman) Peinkofer living with her husband, Joe in Buffalo, NY. They had five children, one son and four daughters. As the author and his wife pulled into their yard, a local Buffalo TV news reporter was waiting, and both Eleanor and the author were interviewed for a news report to be aired on June 6th, the 60th anniversary of D-Day. Later in the day, another interview was conducted along with Frank's sister Mary for the evening Buffalo telecast. On Saturday, June 5th, Eleanor made a presentation to Lynne Belluscio, at the Jell-O Museum. Her presentation described the details of her correspondence with Frank as a grade school child and the lasting impression it made on her. Copies of Frank's letters to her were subsequently placed in the archives of the Jell-O Museum and the Le Roy Historical Society.

The Jell-O Museum in Le Roy, NY continues to honor the servicemen that were employees of the Jell-O Company and served in WWII. A bronze plaque mounted outside the museum lists all of their names with two names, one of which is Frank, listed as killed in action. Further information on the Jell-O Museum can be found at http://www.jellogallery.org

Figure 130 Bronze Plaque Outside Jell-O Museum

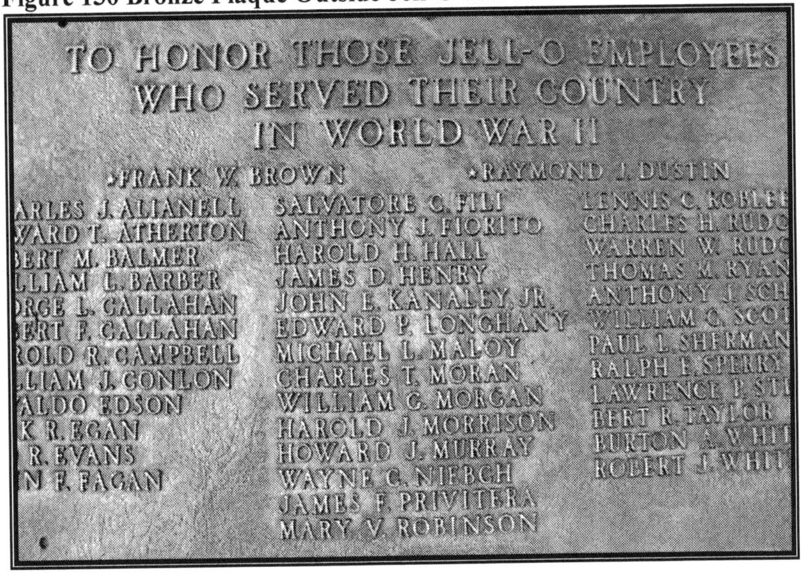

I'm confident the servicemen listed on this plaque were very grateful for the many Jell-O goodwill packages sent to them during that long period of war. The Jell-O Corporation can indeed be proud of their support for the military.

SOLO DEO GLORIA

"****"

194

Notes and Photo Credits

Notes

Chapter 6
 1. Colonel Gerden F. Johnson, History of the Twelfth Infantry Regiment in WWII, 32-33.

Chapter 10
 2. Colonel Gerden F. Johnson, History of the Twelfth Infantry Regiment in   WWII, 39.

Chapter 11
 3. Capt. Marshall O. Becker, The Amphibious Training Center, Study No.22, page 1,57,71, 724.

Chapter 12
 4. Colonel Gerden F. Johnson, History of the Twelfth Infantry Regiment in WWII, 40.

Chapter 13
 5. Colonel Gerden F. Johnson, History of the Twelfth Infantry Regiment in WWII, 41-47
 6. Wikipedia, V-Mail
 7. Colonel Gerden F. Johnson, History of the Twelfth Infantry Regiment in WWII, 47
 8. Wikipedia, Exeter Cathedral
 9. Colonel Gerden F. Johnson, History of the Twelfth Infantry Regiment in WWII, 46
 10. Colonel Gerden F. Johnson, History of the Twelfth Infantry Regiment in WWII, 47-49
 11. Colonel Gerden F. Johnson, History of the Twelfth Infantry Regiment in WWII, 52-54
 12. Ken Small, The Forgotten Dead, 13. Colonel Gerden F. Johnson, History of the Twelfth Infantry Regiment in WWII, 52-54

Chapter 14
 13. Bob Babcock "Deeds Not Words", 4th Infantry Division History, Camp Gordon Johnston Association Web-Site.
 14. Colonel Gerden F. Johnson, History of the Twelfth Infantry Regiment in WWII, 67-71

Photo Credits

All figures, letters and documents in this book are the property of the Frank W. Brown Archives except as follows:

Figure 28 Courtesy of schistorynet/camp croft/
Figure 37 Public Domain
Figure 94 Courtesy of Camp Gordon Johnston Museum
Figure 95 Courtesy of Camp Gordon Johnston Museum
Figure 99 Public Domain
Figure 100 Public Domain
Figure 101 Public Domain
Figure 102 Photo by David Iliff License: CC-BY- SA 3.0
Figure 103 Photo by www.wyrdlight.com, Author Antony McCallum
Figure 105 Public Domain
Figure 107 Wekipedia CC-BY-SA 4.0
Figure 108 Public Domain
Figure 110 Courtesy of Naval History and Heritage Command #80-G-K-2055
Figure 111 Courtesy of Naval History and Heritage Command #80-G-283500
Figure 112 Courtesy of devonww2weebly.com/plymouth
Figure 113 Public Domain
Figure 114 Public Domain
Figure 117 Public Domain
Figure 118 Public Domain
Figure 120 Public Domain
Figure 121 Public Domain
Figure 123 Public Domain

"*****"

Appendix A

Frank's Timeline of Service

May 15 to June 7, 1941	Fort Niagara Induction Center
June 8 to September 19, 1941	Camp Croft, SC
September 21 to October 11, 1941	Fort Devens, MA
October 12 to October 23, 1941	Fort Dix, NJ
October 24 to December 19, 1941	Fort Benning, GA
December 20, '41 to April 11, '43	Camp Gordon, GA
July 7 to July 31, 1942	Carolina Maneuvers
March 11 to March 21, 1943	Maneuvers
April 12 to September 21, 1943	Fort Dix, NJ
September 25 to Nov. 30, 1943	Camp Gordon Johnston, FL
Nov. 30, 1943 to January 9, 1944	Fort Jackson, GA
January 18, 1944 to Jan. 28, 1944	Crossing the Atlantic
January 31, 1944 to June 5, 1944	Exeter, England
June 6, 1944	D-Day Utah Beach
June 8, 1944	Frank Brown KIA
May 22, 1948	Burial St. Francis Cemetery

"****"

Appendix B

Frank's Cartoons

198

199

200

Bill Counting to a 100
1-2-3-4-5-6
7-8-9-10
Bill's snow man
ME
Bill
Snow ball
Bill
dog
Your son
Frank
Bill
HAK
cough
cough
Cough
Blackie

202

203

Blackie is all white Momy
Bill on his skates
Bill
Bill
Bill
Bill
J.H.
Bill fishing
Your son Frank
Bill

Bill digging up the garden
Frank
Bill
dog
FT DIX
Bill speaking his poem to his cat
Your
Bill
Bill
BILL
Bill
mommie can I have a dime

Bill + his stamps

Bill picking
Strawberries

Your son
Frank.
BILL

Bill
Chicken

Bill trying to thread
the needle.

207

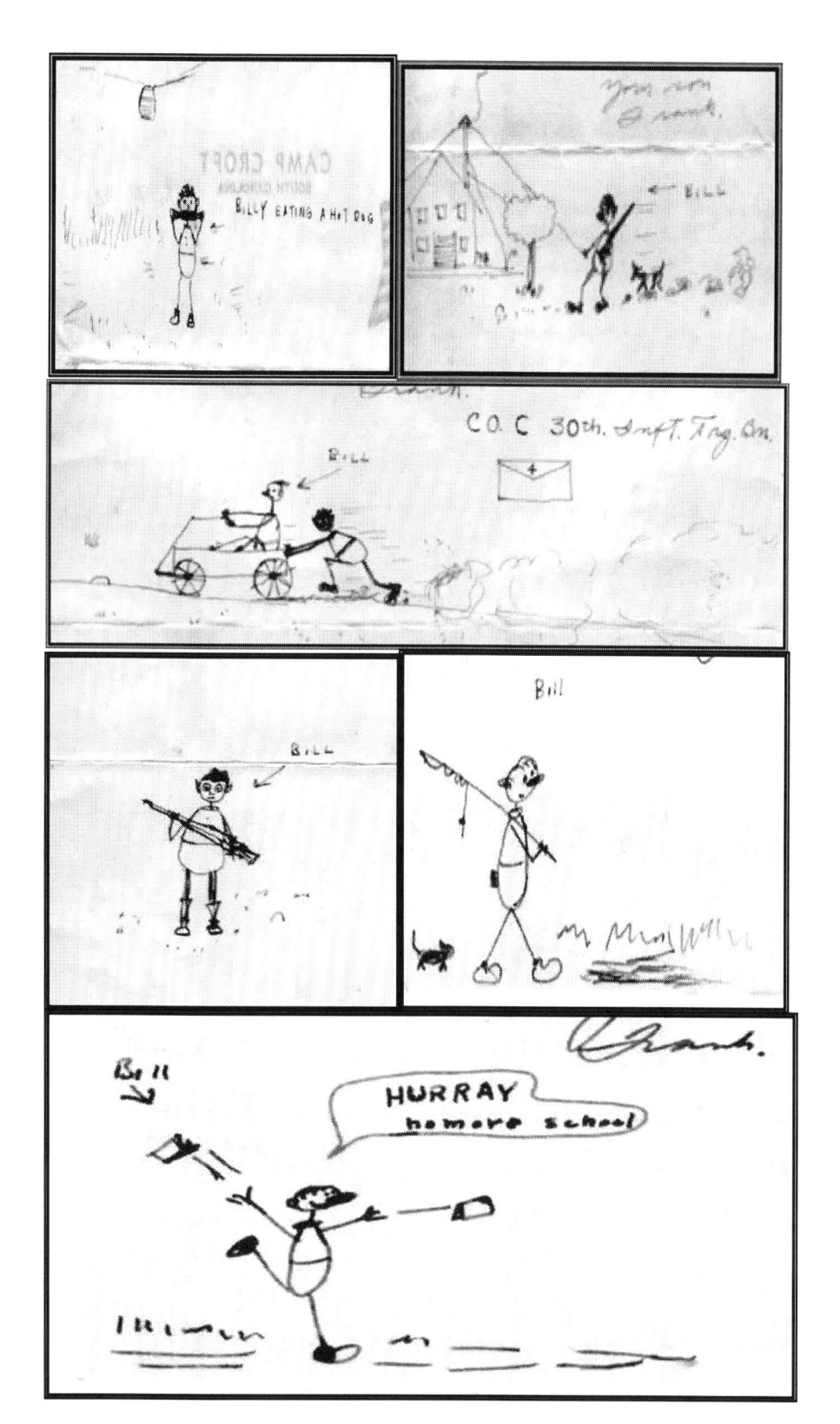

BILL
FEEDING CHICKENS

Bill Feeding the
Monkey at the Zoo

Bill
Ice cream
Cone

Bill

ME

BILL

ME
King
Bill eating watermellon
Bill studying his book
1234
Bill and a fish
Suckers
BILL
CHUCKIE

210

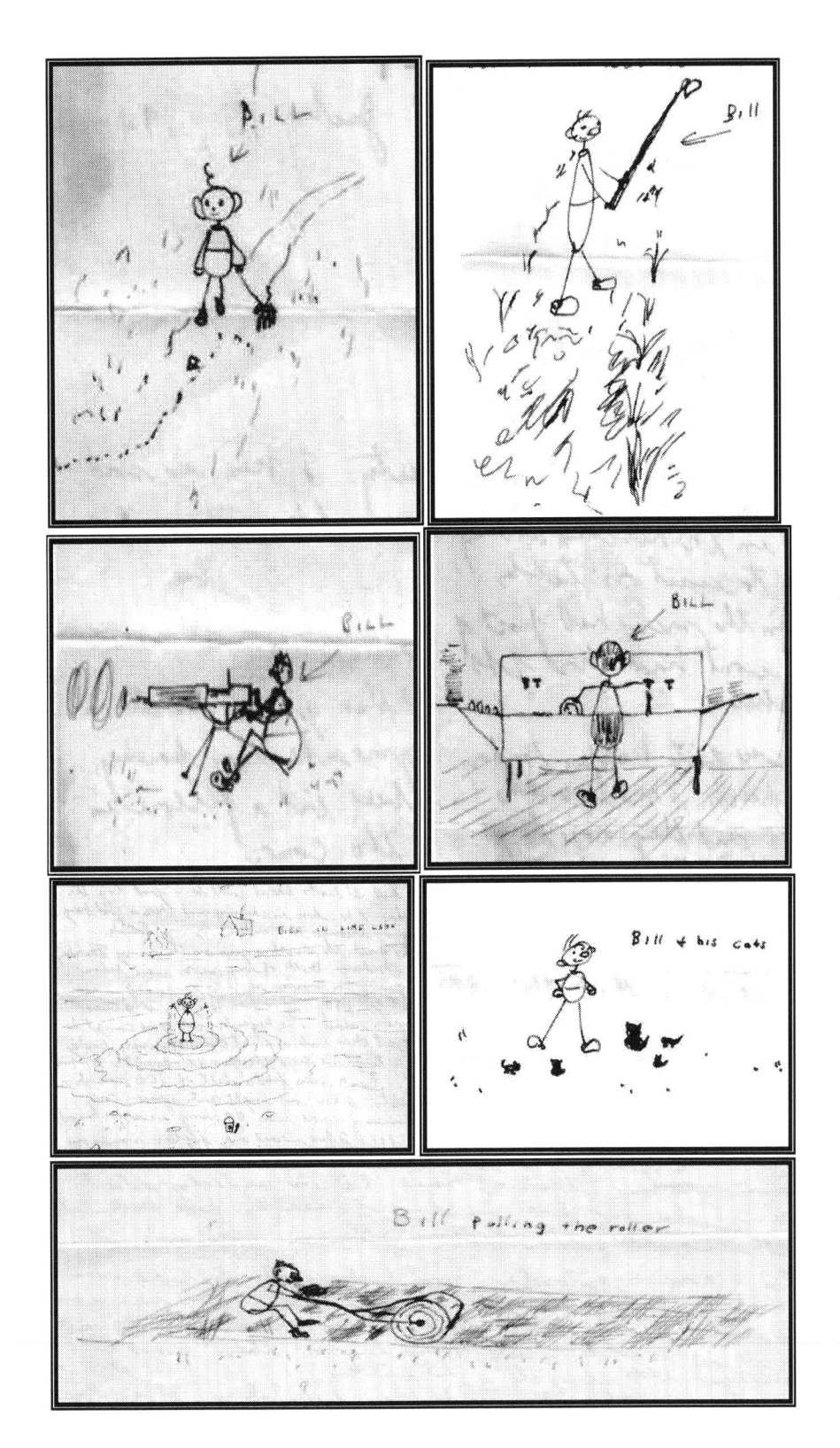

Bill and his dogs

Bill & his Cotton

Bill going to school

Bill & his cats

Bill on Swing

Frank
Bill eating
watermellon

Bill

Bill and one of his teeth

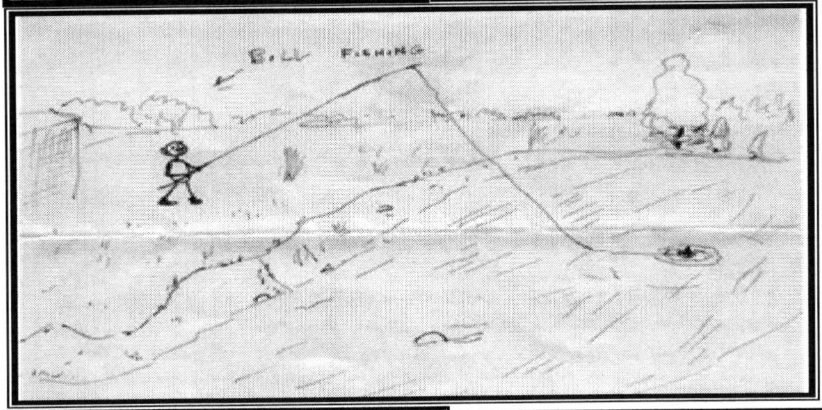
Bill Fishing

Frank
Bill and his cats

Bill

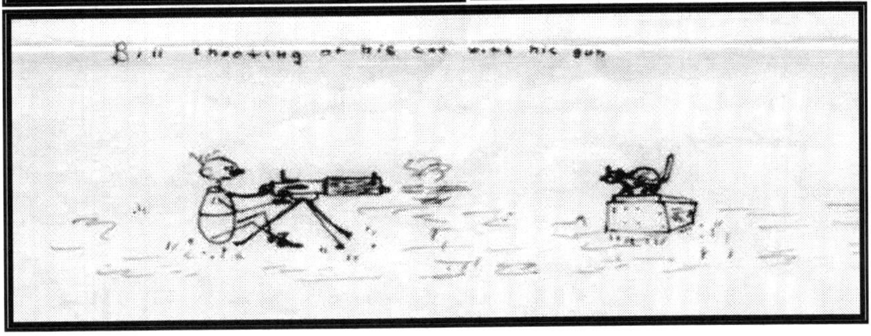
Bill shooting at his cat with his gun

I havent no one to play with
JANE B. has gone to VIRGINIA
Bill
CAT
Bill taking his cat for a ride
Bill taking his cat for a walk
Bill in school
A, B, C, D, E,
1, 2, 3.
Bill

Alfred
NO!
Bill Spelling
Bill running so he wont be late for school
Bill painting a Picture

Bill
books
Blackie

Punkin
Bill
Blackie

Bill

Bill reading a book

Bill
Bill
CAT

Bill writing a letter to SANTA

Bill riding on his sled
Bill rubbing the bump on his head

216

"****"

Appendix C

Letter From Tech. Sgt. Edmund Phillips

Nov. 8, 1947
Secretary, Md.

Dear Mrs Leonard:

    I hardly know how to start this letter. It is true that I was with Leonard almost up until the last which was on the 8th of June. He was a nice clean boy and a very good soldier. We spent the last week or so in a marshalling area which is a place where we were all restricted for security reasons and briefed. We had lots of spare time so we spent it playing soft ball and volley ball. We also did lots of writing home as we knew something was going to happen. From here we were put aboard a boat (L.C.S) We stayed on the boat until D Day morning. Most of this time on the boat was spent getting equipment ready, last minute instructions and sleeping. We hit the beach at 10:30 o'clock. We made it across the beach and the next day, without any casualties in our platoon. On the morning of the 8th we got ready to push off after not much sleep the first two nights. We met plenty of resistance that morning and kept on moving right through it.

    The last I saw Bob he was acting as first scout and was telling our squad leader, who was also killed, what he saw up ahead of him. Now that was when I was wounded and was evacuated to England. I later returned to the Company and learned about all the casualties we suffered that day which was over 2/3 of the Company. A fellow by the name of Crocker from Tennessee told me that Bob was killed along side him and it was so quick and sudden that there was no pain at all. Well that is all I can tell you. I hope I havent said or told you something I shouldnt so as to wrorry you I feel that mothers paid as big a price, as, or more than anyone in this past war. You asked about what money Bob had. Well we checked our money into the company commander and he in turn left it in England with headquarters. Whether he had any money I dont know. You will have to excuse my writing . I dont get much practice since I have left the Army.

    I hope I have answered some of your questions and if anytime I can help by telling you som thing or giving you some information, please write.

                      Sincerely

                        Edmund F Phillips.

"*****"

Appendix D

Letter from Lt. Forbes

(Note: This letter was typed from the original handwritten letter to enable ease of reading)

5 Mar 45

My Dear Miss Brown,

I wish acknowledge the receipt of your letter regarding your Brothers death. I think I can give you a little information. I can certainly appreciate your anxiety and the confusion caused by the official communications.

Our company was in the vicinity of Montebourg in Normandy when the Germans threw a heavy counterattack at us. In this action a large number of the company was lost. In this action Sgt. Brown displayed bravery and courage this is not found in the common man. It was indeed a thing to be remembered. After the action we took again the ground we had lost and recovered the dead and wounded. This was on the 8th of June.

I consider it a great honor to have fought beside your brother. I do hope you can fine some small consolation in knowing that he died a brave man and he was one of the finest men I have known. If I can be of further service to you an your family, do not hesitate to let me know.

If you hear from the other men in the company, I would consider it a personal favor if you would let me know how they are.

Hoping this will rest your mind, I remain-
    Your Servant,
    William A. Forbes
    1st Lt. Inf.
    (Ltr. from Lt. Wm. A. Forbes 0-132415C, Hq. G.F.O.T.C., Academic Dept.,
    A.P.O. 545, c/o PM, N.Y., N.Y.)

Handwritten Letter From Lt. William Forbes
5 March 1945

5 Mar. 45

My Dear Miss Brown,

I wish acknowledge the receipt of your letter regarding your Brothers death.

I think I can give you a little information. I can certainly appreciate your anxiety and the confusion caused by the official communications.

Our company was in the vicinity of Martleburg in Normandy when the Germans threw a heavy counterattack at us. In this action a large number of the company was lost. In this action Sgt Brown displayed bravery and courage this is not found in the common man. It was indeed a thing to be remembered.

After the action we took again the ground we had lost and recovered the dead and wounded. This was on the 8th of June.

I consider it a great honor to have fought beside your brother. I do hope you can find some small consolation in knowing that he died a brave man and he was one of the finest men

220

I have ever known.

If I can be of further service to you or your family, do not hesitate to let me know.

If you hear from the other men in the company I would consider it a personal favor if you would let me know how they are.

Hoping this will rest your mind, I remain

Your Servant,
William H. Forbes
Lt.

Lt. Wm. H. Forbes O-1324410
Hq. C.E.O.T.C., Academic Dept.
A.P.O. 545
% PM, N.Y., N.Y.

U.S. ARMY POSTAL SERVICE
545
MAR 6
1945
A.P.O.

Miss Mary J. Brown
R.D. 2
LeRoy, N.Y.

Wm. H. Forbes
Lt.

"*****"

About the Author

The author is the brother of Frank W. Brown and knew him as a child during WWII. He is a graduate of the University of Buffalo, School of Engineering and served in the USAF for three years at Wright Air Research & Development Command followed by 33 years at the NASA Glenn (Lewis) Research Center. He authored several technical papers and the Hydrogen & Oxygen Safety Manuals, retiring in 1993. He has been married to his wife Mary Ann for 56 years, has four sons: Frank, Richard, Robert, Christopher, 12 grandchildren, and two great-grandchildren.

HURON PUBLIC LIBRARY
333 WILLIAMS STREET
HURON, OHIO 44839

Made in the USA
Middletown, DE
21 June 2016